100 Experiential Learning Activities

for Social Studies, Literature, and the Arts, Grades 5-12

100 Experiential Learning Activities

for Social Studies, Literature, and the Arts, Grades 5-12

Eugene F.
PROVENZO, JR.

Dan W.
BUTIN

Anthony
ANGELINI

 **CORWIN PRESS**
A SAGE Company
Thousand Oaks, CA 91320

Copyright © 2008 by Corwin Press

For information:

Corwin Press
A Sage Publications Company
2455 Teller Road
Thousand Oaks, California 91320
www.corwinpress.com

Sage Publications Ltd.
1 Oliver's Yard
55 City Road
London EC1Y 1SP
United Kingdom

Sage Publications India Pvt. Ltd.
B 1/I 1 Mohan Cooperative Industrial Area
Mathura Road, New Delhi 110 044
India

Sage Publications Asia-Pacific Pte. Ltd.
33 Pekin Street #02–01
Far East Square
Singapore 048763

Printed in the United States of America.

Library of Congress Cataloging-in-Publication Data

Provenzo, Eugene F.
100 experiential learning activities for social studies, literature, and the arts, grades 5–12 / Eugene F. Provenzo Jr., Dan W. Butin, Anthony Angelini.
        p. cm.
Includes bibliographical references and index.
ISBN 978-1-4129-3999-7 (cloth)
ISBN 978-1-4129-4000-9 (pbk.)

    1. Experiential learning. 2. Active learning. 3. Middle school education—Activity programs. 4. Education, Secondary—Activity programs. I. Butin, Dan W. (Dan Wernaa) II. Angelini, Anthony. III. Title. IV. Title: One hundred experiential learning activities for social studies, literature, and the arts, grades 5–12.

LB1027.23.P76 2008
371.39—dc22   2007050193

This book is printed on acid-free paper.

08   09   10   11   12   10   9   8   7   6   5   4   3   2   1

Senior Acquisitions Editor:	Debra Stollenwerk
Editorial Assistants:	Lesley Blake, Allison Scott, and Gem Rabanera
Production Editor:	Veronica Stapleton
Copy Editor:	Linda Gray
Typesetter:	C&M Digitals (P) Ltd.
Proofreader:	Andrea Martin
Graphic Designer:	Lisa Riley

Table of Contents

Preface

This book is a professional collaboration that grew out of our mutual interest in experiential learning. While attending the American Educational Research Association meeting several years ago in Chicago, Dan and Gene met for dinner. Dan explained that he was interested in writing a book on experiential learning. Gene said he had been collecting materials for a hands-on set of learning experiences that were based on many of the teaching methods he used in his undergraduate classes at the University of Miami and that he felt they could easily be adapted for use in middle school and high school. We decided that we could collaborate on the creation of a book.

Over the course of the next two years, we exchanged materials. Dan articulated the book's general philosophy as reflected in the Introduction to this book, and Gene concentrated on the activities. Anthony Angelini, a former student of Dan's at Gettysburg College and now a high school social studies teacher, worked with Dan to critique and revise the activities in the book and to develop the curriculum matrices for each activity.

Eugene F. Provenzo, Jr., University of Miami
Dan Butin, Cambridge College

Acknowledgments

Our editors at Corwin Press, Faye Zucker and Deb Stollenwerk, provided us with encouragement and support throughout this project, as did our families. Special thanks go to Asterie Baker Provenzo for help with final editing and proofing. Also thanks go to Faye's assistant, Gem Rabanera, who helped with illustrations, formatting issues, and the usual questions that come up in getting a book into final production.

Corwin Press would like to thank the following individuals for their contributions to the work:

Jerome I. Leventhal
Professor Emeritus
Temple University Department of Curriculum, Instruction, and
    Technology in Education
Philadelphia, PA

India Meissel
Lead Teacher
Lakeland High School
Suffolk, VA

Daniel K. Thompson
Assistant Professor
Penn State University
University Park, PA

David C. Virtue
Assistant Professor
University of South Carolina
Columbia, SC

About the Authors

Eugene F. Provenzo, Jr. is a professor in the Department of Teaching and Learning, School of Education, University of Miami. He is the author of more than fifty books on education, computing, history, and culture, including *Video Kids: Making Sense of Nintendo* (1991) and *Critical Literacy: What Every American Ought to Know* (2005). With Sage Publications, he is the editor of *Critical Issues in Education* (2006) and is editor-in-chief of Sage's forthcoming *Encyclopedia of the Social and Cultural Foundations of Education* (anticipated publication fall 2008).

Source: Kim Indresano Photography.

Dan W. Butin is an associate professor and assistant dean of Cambridge College's school of education. He is the editor of *Service-Learning in Higher Education* (2005) and *Teaching Social Foundations of Education* (2005), and author of a forthcoming book (from Corwin Press) on how to complete a timely and rigorous dissertation in education. Dr. Butin is an editorial board member of the journal *Educational Studies*. His research focuses on issues of educator preparation and policy and active learning strategies in higher education. Prior to working in higher education, Dr. Butin taught middle school in an adult GED program and was the chief financial officer of Teacher For America. More about Dr. Butin's teaching and research can be found at http://danbutin.org/.

Anthony Angelini is a graduate of Gettysburg College where he worked as a research assistant to Dr. Dan Butin, one of the results of which is this book. He is now a social studies teacher at Gettysburg Area High School working with students of various grade levels.

Introduction

In *Teaching to Transgress*, bell hooks (1994) offers a vivid metaphor of active learning. Quoting a Buddhist writer, she depicts the exuberance of teaching as

> preparing for groundlessness, preparing for the reality of human existence, you are living on the razor's edge . . . things are not certain and they do not last and you do not know what is going to happen. My teachers have always pushed me over the cliff. (p. 207)

For her, teaching is about pushing boundaries, examining unthinking and unthinkable positions, and guiding students through a perilous, tumultuous, and exhilarating intellectual journey.

But how do we do that? How do teachers create spaces for learning where students become engaged and motivated to participate and learn? How do we develop truly dynamic learning environments within the constraints of the classroom? Educational researchers have long spoken about the middle and high school classroom as a place of passive learning and disconnected knowledge (Cuban, 1992; Goodlad, 1984). The hidden curriculum of schooling (Jackson, 1990) fosters and prioritizes teacher-centered, textbook-driven, time-parceled, classroom-bounded, and goal-directed learning rather than deep and sustained student learning.

Yet contemporary educational researchers are able to provide extremely useful insights for creating positive classroom environments (Bransford, 2000). For example, students learn when they are able to see the "big picture" rather than when they are just given a set of disconnected facts, when they are engaged in their learning rather than positioned as passive spectators, and when they believe that such learning leads to meaningful outcomes rather than to predefined and predetermined goals.

WHY THIS BOOK: A "ROAD MAP" OR GUIDE FOR CREATING EXPERIENTIAL LEARNING ACTIVITIES IN SOCIAL STUDIES AND HUMANITIES

What is all too often absent is a detailed "road map" that can guide teachers toward creating such learning opportunities. This book provides just such a resource for teachers who want to begin to move beyond traditional models of teaching and learning in the social studies, literature, and the arts. It is grounded in the well-documented reality that students learn by engaging—deeply, passionately, and inquisitively—with content knowledge (Meier, 2002; Schwartz, Lin, Brophy, & Bransford, 2003) and that such learning not only enhances one's academic achievement but offers opportunities to think differently about how we see ourselves and the world. Moreover, such active learning facilitates the realization that our classrooms and our local and global communities are not so distant from each other—that, in fact, we can make a difference by learning to think and feel and act differently.

This is, after all, at the heart of the mission and vision of the humanities and social sciences: to help students delve into primary sources, construct careful arguments, question deeply held assumptions, and encounter a fundamentally foreign idea or culture. These are all enactments of genuine thinking and learning. To do this effectively, though, teachers must be given adequate scaffolding. We know from our own and our students' experiences that teaching and learning "outside the box" is an uncomfortable process requiring additional preparation, rethinking teaching strategies, and overcoming implicit normative boundaries of what a classroom is supposed to look like.

Yet we believe that it is also something that people can be shown how to do. We have seen many of our colleagues, our students, and our student-teachers begin to rethink how they teach and how their students learn. This does not occur from a spontaneous realization. Rather, we have helped our students and our colleagues realize the step-by-step process necessary for developing powerfully engaging classroom practices.

This is, in fact, exactly the purpose of this book. We provide 100 experiential learning activities that can support students' deep and sustained learning. These activities range across numerous disciplines—history, economics, literature, and the arts—such that they can be used in many types of middle and high school classes. We have focused on these areas (rather than, for example, on math and sciences) exactly because we have found that teachers need support to engage students' critical thinking and reflection around oftentimes complex, ambiguous, and contested content knowledge.

Each activity is structured with a short introduction for the teacher, followed by the actual activity (and accompanying materials for photocopying if relevant) for the students to do. This format allows teachers quick access to a thought-through and detailed learning activity that can be brought forth at the most appropriate classroom moment. We have worked hard to create these learning activities so that they are applicable across both middle and high school classes. You, the teacher, will of course have to judge your own students' level to slightly modify the activities accordingly. We have found, for example, that middle school students may better benefit from having the teacher explain the introductory contextual materials, whereas high school students can oftentimes gain much from reading it themselves.

A critical feature of this book is that we have consciously and systematically linked every single activity to the relevant national standards in the social studies, literature, and the arts (through the McREL and National Council of Social Studies [NCSS] standards). We have thus constructed two matrices (that can be found at the end of this introduction) that list every single activity and the relevant standards that are met. Almost all the activities, it should be noted, meet more than one particular standard or substandard. An activity may thus be applicable for both the Civics and Historical Understanding standards; and within Historical Understanding, an activity may be applicable for both the substandards of understanding the historical perspective and how to analyze chronological relationships and patterns.

This format should be of great help to teachers attempting to align their classroom work with the relevant and applicable standards in their daily lesson planning. We envision that teachers can skim through the matrices to find a particular standard that needs to be taught and thus easily view which activities best meet such standards. Moreover, such a format allows teachers the opportunity to bring in multidisciplinary content and multiple intelligences since many activities meet several standards and can be done through diverse mediums. Because of this, we have not attempted to organize the activities in a particular order (such as chronologically) because there are so many ways that each activity can be taught and standards that it can meet.

We hope that it is by now clear that this book is not simply a compilation of "icebreakers" or generic ideas for "activating" student engagement. While such activities are sometimes useful in particular situations, we believe that true learning occurs through the in-depth and systematic engagement with specific complex issues and dilemmas. Moreover, teachers can benefit from detailed articulations of how to enact active learning strategies. Nearly all the activities included in this book have been used in one form or another in our classrooms. Some of the examples are drawn loosely from models we have found with other teachers. In those cases, where we have gotten an idea from an outside source, we have reworked the activity in new ways, often merging it with another activity, or putting a new twist on it. We are confident that nearly all these activities will work well in most classroom settings.

We must of course acknowledge that what works for us and our students may not work for you. Classrooms are always site specific, with myriad contextual markers that affect teaching and learning. Yet it is possible to transfer good ideas if one is sensitive to the specific context and goals where such ideas are used. Just as we all tell the same joke in slightly different ways and with slightly different variations depending on the audience and situation, so too will these experiential activities have slightly different formats. While the punch line may be the same, the delivery, as always, is up to you.

WHY THESE ACTIVITIES?

Before beginning to use this book, we believe it is important that you also have a bigger picture of why we have chosen the activities that we did and formatted them in the way that we have. Specifically, the activities we have created focus on issues of *meaning making, paradigm shifting,* and *self-understanding.* These, we believe, are critical aspects of truly developing and enacting active learning in a classroom.

Meaning Making

By *meaning making,* we are referring to the process by which people come to understand the world around them. Research across a variety of fields—from cognitive science to learning theory to anthropology—suggests that humans are extremely adept at pattern making and pattern perceiving. In Clifford Geertz's (1973) oft-cited phrasing, we are ensconced within "webs of meaning." As such, we learn things by relating them to prior knowledge and experience, by contextualizing such knowledge in specific situations, and by being able to generalize and transfer such knowledge across conditions. This happens whether we are teaching about different cultures, past civilizations, or economic principles.

Two classic examples will make this clear. The first comes from expert–novice research. Researchers have shown that what separates chess masters from novice players is not the master player's ability to more quickly work through all the possible moves on the board and their long-term consequences (technically referred to as the greater breadth and depth of search); rather, chess masters were much more adept at "chunking" chess configurations and thus knowing quickly which were fruitful for further consideration. While novices spent equal time working through as many possible moves as time allowed, chess masters immediately focused on the limited set of moves they deemed relevant for the situation at hand (DeGroot, 1965). What is revealing is that such chunking works only when the configurations are "real." Researchers asked master and novice players to reconstruct the position of randomly set-up chess figures after glancing at a board for five seconds. When the configurations mirrored possible meaningful game positions, master players' recall was dramatically better than novices; yet when the configurations were truly random, masters and novices did just as poorly (Chase & Simon, 1973).

A second example comes from research on transferring learning. A group of researchers (Ericsson, Chase, & Faloon, 1980) worked with a college student on memorizing randomly generated digit strings. By chunking such numbers into meaningful combinations (e.g., telephone numbers, or in this student's case, winning times for famous track races), the student was able to memorize up to seventy numbers in a row. Yet when presented with a series of randomly generated letter strings, the student did just as poorly (up to seven in a row) as before he had started practicing.

Learning thus seems to be supported by generating ever-expanding frameworks for knowledge. We remember things, be it chess positions or random numbers, if they are meaningful to us. They are meaningful to us if they are framed within our prior knowledge (such as past chess games or track times), and if they help us make sense of our present situation. Interestingly, and this presages the discussion on self-understanding, this does not work if the meaning making is simply a set of rules to follow, such as was the case of the college student's memorization. If the student was given the metaperspective of how chunking enhances memory, he might have been able to come up with meaningful ways to chunk the randomly generated letters; instead, he only knew how to memorize numbers.

Meaning making is thus about providing specific "big ideas" that allow students to make meaning of the specific knowledge to be learned. These big ideas serve as foundations for learning; they are stories, metaphors, and narratives that serve as points of departure (and return) by which we can weave webs of relationships and connections to a multitude of seemingly disparate data. This occurs in every class—think of the "big bang" in physics, the "march of progress" in history, or the golden ratio in art history—and offers both novices and experts guidance in their research and comprehension (with experts, obviously, treating such "grand narratives" as stories to argue with rather than simply accept).

Many of these activities emphasize the "big" issues within middle and high school classes. We specifically focus on issues of culture, language, diversity, arts and artifacts, economics, and science and technology. By actively and deeply grappling with the specific issues in each activity, students come to better understand the idea's assumptions and implications in a very real and personal way. They are of course ultimately free to embrace, modify, or reject the idea. But what they cannot do is ignore it. Stories and metaphors live with us and in us, or as Basso (2000) nicely phrases it, stories "stalk us," forcing us to struggle with them until we make peace by deciding who we are in relation to the story. Meaning-making activities hope to do exactly that: to offer students a means to work through their notions of who they are and what they believe within the context of very specific big issues in their classrooms.

Paradigm Shifting

Many of our activities are also about paradigm shifting. We all live with big ideas. All too often, however, they are implicit ideas that we have never explicitly acknowledged, much less examined or carefully thought through. Sometimes this examination of our "folk beliefs" offers the opportunity to more fully embrace our own or someone else's ideas. Yet the issues brought out in the humanities and social sciences are complex and multifaceted and often have profound and far-reaching social, cultural, and political consequences. The examination of such "contested knowledge" is therefore frequently resisted (Butin, 2005). Our students are, unfortunately, all too often content with their unacknowledged and unexamined assumptions and beliefs. They, in other words, don't want to shift their paradigms.

Howard Gardner (2004) has recently written about how we actually go about changing people's minds. He suggests that we come to change our perspectives and actions through reasoning and research, personal and real-world resonance, and the representational vividness of new ideas. But even with such foreknowledge, it is a difficult undertaking to overcome students' active and passive resistance. We resist new ideas because we do not want to change who we are. We are unwilling (or afraid) to walk in another's shoes—because to do so would put into doubt the legitimacy and stability of our own self-conception. For our students, the only entrance into genuine and difficult discussions is through active engagement with alternative models of how the world may be different.

Paradigm shifting is not an easy act; as such, many activities in this book employ a host of stratagems to help students overcome their resistance to change. For students begin with the notion that the world is a stable, static, and ultimately knowable place. They believe that teachers can give them all the right answers in fifty-minute increments across their middle and high school life. Yet the classroom as we envision it and as we enact it becomes a place where students must grapple with their own (and their teachers') sense of how to understand the world and our relationship to it.

John Dewey (1910) suggested that all true learning begins with a condition of doubt, a "forked-road" situation, "which is ambiguous, which presents a dilemma . . . [which] involves willingness to endure a condition of mental unrest and disturbance" (pp. 11, 13). It is only in such disturbance of the normal and seemingly "natural," Dewey argued, that deep assumptions become visible, that paradigmatic perspectives shift, that our expectations are redefined.

Similarly, the activities in this book embrace Dewey's criterion of a forked-road situation. They create a condition of doubt, they open a wedge in the seeming solidity and stability of unexamined assumptions, and they question the foundations of what we consider "real." We must of course remember that such acts are not to be taken lightly. As the educational philosopher James Garrison (1998, quoted in Abowitz, 2005) has commented,

> In my classes I am effectively telling some good people to abandon the beliefs and values of just about everyone and everything they love. You cannot do such a thing and confidently predict it will always come out well. Remember, our beliefs and values are who we are, they are embodied and held passionately; they constitute our very identities. Have you ever heard the sound of your dearest value breaking? (p. 133)

As we introduce new perspectives and paradigms, we must therefore also remember that we can never create learning. We can only set the occasion. We can bring students to the edge, work to create the "aha" moment, and offer them a meaningful alternative on the other side. Yet we cannot force students across the insurmountable chasm that separates where they are and where we want them to go. That is, in a sense, an existential leap of faith.

The activities we have included in this book can be thought of as constructing the conditions for such leaps or border crossings. Paradigm-shifting activities offer students the opportunity to begin to visualize, understand, and enact the assumptions and implications of different paradigms. We therefore focus on issues of rituals, symbols, power, and authority. Each of these issues links across multiple fields, multiple histories, and multiple cultures. As such, students come to understand that shifting paradigms is about learning to accept a fundamentally different way of looking at the world; this can be done, we suggest, only by engaging these topics through deep and sustained activities. This does not occur immediately or completely. But it can be facilitated by engaging on multiple levels—cognitively, affectively, and psychologically—with particular far-reaching perspectives. Our activities attempt to provide such immersion opportunities.

Self-Understanding

Finally, our activities are about self-understanding. Self-understanding can be thought of as the ability for reflection, self-regulation, and critical thinking about our own beliefs and actions. Research on such "metacognition" (Brown, Collins, & Durgid, 1989) demonstrates that individuals who reflect on and understand their learning strengths and weaknesses, and modify their actions accordingly, are much better at accomplishing new or variant tasks. Moreover, metacognitive strategies are critical for fostering productive "habits of mind" (Wiggins & McTighe, 1998) that emphasize self-initiated and self-engaged learners.

On a deeper level, self-understanding can be thought of as a type of metalearning, or what Gregory Bateson (2000) termed "deutro-learning." Bateson argued that we should study not only how people learn but how people learn to learn. How do we come to understand the metaphenomena that guide particular incidents (such as an apple falling out of a tree)? How do we organize knowledge (about myths or random digit strings) so that we can seamlessly integrate new knowledge?

The difference in these levels of learning can be distinguished between being proficient or even an expert in a particular thing (be it chess, European history, or memorizing random digit strings) and being able to apply such mastery to an ever-expanding set of analogous situations. Michael Huberman (1993) offers a vivid depiction of the teacher as artisan that speaks to such a conceptualization of the virtuoso. The teacher-as-artisan, Huberman argues, works through a process of "bricolage," taking ideas and materials from a host of sources and combining them in unique combinations to suit the particularities of the specific classroom situation. Like the jazz musician, teachers-as-artisans can draw on a deep reserve of content and process knowledge to quickly develop the appropriate rhythm and structure to "go with the flow" of what is happening around them, be it in a jazz quintet or with twenty-four college-bound seniors.

What teachers-as-artisans and virtuoso jazz musicians have is the self-understanding of their capacities and the limitations and possibilities of such capacities. Virtuoso teachers do not try to push their students too far or too fast; on the other hand, they know exactly what they need to do to push students and support them to the limits of their abilities.

How we conceive of ourselves—our cognitive abilities, our physical attributes, our personalities—may be drastically different from how others see us or how we may actually perform. By beginning to develop a nuanced sense of what we do and how we think, we are able to foster and extend our capacities for reflection and action. Our activities for self-understanding attempt to engage such issues directly; we examine self-understanding by engaging students in experiential learning activities about our historical, social, cultural, political, and global contexts. All these examples help us confront our notion of who we are and want to be.

We therefore hope that this book provides you with both the foundation and the road map necessary to develop engaging and thought-provoking experiential learning activities that can extend your own classroom work. These activities cannot substitute for the specific content and context of your specific course. Nor are they meant to.

We use these activities, and others like them, in our own classrooms as a means to facilitate and clarify our particular content-specific discussions and debates. They offer us a means to "switch gears," to reframe conversations a little too stuck, to push our students just a little further than a regular classroom give-and-take usually does. Sometimes these activities are planned far in advance. Sometimes we "pull them out of our back pockets" when we see a teachable moment.

Regardless of the specific situation, though, these activities help our teaching become a little more alive by engaging students' hearts and minds. Sometimes they bring us to the edge of bell hook's vision of engaged pedagogy. Sometimes they simply help us make a point. But what they always do is remind us that teaching and learning are infuriatingly complex, are extremely dynamic, and forever impact our sense of who we are and what we do. We hope that this book provides numerous opportunities to engage with this vision of the classroom.

Matrices

Matrix of Activities Correlated to the National Council of Social Studies (NCSS) Standards

	Activity	I Culture	II Time, Continuity, & Change	III People, Places, & Environments	IV Individual Development & Identity	V Individuals, Groups, & Institutions	VI Power, Authority, & Governance	VII Production, Distribution, & Consumption	VIII Science, Technology, & Society	IX Global Connections	X Civic Ideals & Practices
1	Creating a Language	x				x					
2	Point-of-View Pictures	x	x		x	x					
3	Rosie the Riveter	x	x		x		x	x	x		
4	Columbus and the Discovery of the New World	x	x						x	x	
5	How Is History Portrayed?	x	x				x				
6	Spanglish	x		x	x						
7	Slave Narratives	x	x	x			x				
8	The Paradox of Theseus's Ship		x				x		x		
9	Creating a Personal Historical Timeline		x		x						
10	Poems Inspired by Art	x			x						
11	Art Inspired by Poetry	x			x						
12	The Paradox of Infinity		x						x		
13	Point of View and Cultural Perspectives	x		x			x			x	
14	The Final Flight of Yamamoto	x								x	x
15	Double Consciousness				x	x					x
16	The Fable of the Blind Men and the Elephant		x							x	x

	Activity	I Culture	II Time, Continuity, & Change	III People, Places, & Environments	IV Individual Development & Identity	V Individuals, Groups, & Institutions	VI Power, Authority, & Governance	VII Production, Distribution, & Consumption	VIII Science, Technology, & Society	IX Global Connections	X Civic Ideals & Practices
17	Creating a System of Writing					x			x	x	
18	Magic and Technology		x	x					x		
19	The Birthday Paradox					x					
20	Möbius Strip and Different Perspectives								x		
21	Thinking Out of the Paradigm		x		x					x	
22	Arthur C. Clarke's First Law		x		x				x		
23	Is Technology Neutral?		x		x				x		
24	Writing a Letter to the Editor	x									x
25	Science Fiction and Literature as the Future		x						x		
26	Creating a Political Broadside		x			x	x		x		
27	Exploring the Great Depression	x	x	x							
28	Family Photographs		x	x							
29	Women's Rights	x	x				x				
30	Today in History		x		x						x
31	Photographs of the Farm Security Administration		x	x			x		x		
32	Primary and Secondary Sources		x			x					
33	Thinking Outside the Box		x		x					x	

(Continued)

	Activity	I Culture	II Time, Continuity, & Change	III People, Places, & Environments	IV Individual Development & Identity	V Individuals, Groups, & Institutions	VI Power, Authority, & Governance	VII Production, Distribution, & Consumption	VIII Science, Technology, & Society	IX Global Connections	X Civic Ideals & Practices
34	Riddles		x		x						
35	Exploring Community Festivals			x		x				x	x
36	Rebuses and Concrete Writing	x									
37	Mnemonics				x						
38	Designing a Memorial			x		x					
39	Stepping Into a Painting	x	x		x						
40	Japanese Internment During World War II	x	x			x	x				x
41	ASCII Code								x		
42	Protest Songs	x		x			x				x
43	Inaugural Presidential Address						x				x
44	Portals to the World	x		x						x	
45	Stories From Childhood		x	x		x					
46	Round-Robin Stories				x						
47	Writing Grab Bag				x						
48	Using Census Data		x	x			x				
49	Explore a Favorite Artist				x						
50	What Makes a Good Life?	x			x						x

	Activity	I Culture	II Time, Continuity, & Change	III People, Places, & Environments	IV Individual Development & Identity	V Individuals, Groups, & Institutions	VI Power, Authority, & Governance	VII Production, Distribution, & Consumption	VIII Science, Technology, & Society	IX Global Connections	X Civic Ideals & Practices
51	Creating an Ethical Will		x		x						
52	Written in Stone	x	x	x							
53	Photographic Timeline	x	x	x							
54	1900		x					x	x		
55	95 Theses	x					x				
56	Analyzing *The New England Primer*		x			x			x		x
57	Slavery in the Constitution?		x				x				x
58	How Crowded Was the Middle Passage?			x		x	x				
59	The List			x		x					
60	Sacrifices	x		x	x						x
61	The Classroom Missile Crisis			x			x			x	
62	Listening to Sources?				x	x			x		
63	Personal Timelines	x	x		x	x					
64	Movies as a Window Into History	x		x							
65	Writing Their Own Script	x		x		x					
66	Write Your Own Obituary		x			x					

(Continued)

(Continued)

	Activity	I Culture	II Time, Continuity, & Change	III People, Places, & Environments	IV Individual Development & Identity	V Individuals, Groups, & Institutions	VI Power, Authority, & Governance	VII Production, Distribution, & Consumption	VIII Science, Technology, & Society	IX Global Connections	X Civic Ideals & Practices
67	Take a Trip to Mars								x		
68	CIA Fact Book			x			x				
69	Talking to an Expert										x
70	Famous Last Words								x		
71	Columbus and Culture		x	x		x					x
72	Collage				x	x					
73	Making Models								x		
74	The World Without Human Life		x	x							
75	Creating the Scene for a Story	x		x							
76	How Long Is a Thousand Years?		x								
77	Creating a Dadaist Poem				x						
78	War Stories	x		x							
79	Editorial Cartoons as Social Commentary										x
80	True or False			x		x				x	
81	Creating Codes	x				x					
82	What Is the Law?										x
83	When Is the Law the Law?										x

	Activity	I Culture	II Time, Continuity, & Change	III People, Places, & Environments	IV Individual Development & Identity	V Individuals, Groups, & Institutions	VI Power, Authority, & Governance	VII Production, Distribution, & Consumption	VIII Science, Technology, & Society	IX Global Connections	X Civic Ideals & Practices
84	Symbols in Our Culture	x		x							
85	Symbols on Our Money	x									
86	What's on the Stamp?	x		x							
87	Place Names			x							
88	Art Museums of the World	x									
89	America's Attic	x									
90	Written in Stone			x		x					
91	Photographic Timeline		x	x	x						
92	The Sounds of Silence				x						
93	What's in a Name?	x		x	x					x	
94	More What's in a Name?	x		x	x	x	x				
95	Crazy Inventions								x		
96	Idioms	x								x	
97	Famous Inventions and Their Impact on the World		x						x		
98	What Is in Good Taste?	x		x		x			x		
99	Creating a Self-Portrait				x						
100	Found Art	x							x		

NCSS standards available at http://www.socialstudies.org/standards/strands/

Matrix of Activities Correlated to the Mid-continent Research for Education and Learning (McREL) Standards

	Activity	Behavior Studies	Civics	Economics	Geography	Historical Understanding	United States History	World History	Language Arts	Science	Visual Arts	Mathematics	Self-Regulation	Music	Thinking & Reasoning
1	Creating a Language	2:3, 2:4							6:1, 6:7						
2	Point-of-View Pictures					1:1, 2:9, 2:11									
3	Rosie the Riveter	4:1, 4:5	11:3				25:4	41:3							
4	Columbus and the Discovery of the New World				9:4	2:1, 2:8, 2:13	2:3, 2:4	29:4							
5	How Is History Portrayed?				9:4	2:1, 2:8, 2:13	2:3, 2:4	29:4							
6	Spanglish	4:11	14:2				31:1, 31:2, 31:5	45:2							
7	Slave Narratives					2:10, 2:11	10:2, 10:3, 10:6, 13:2, 24:2	40:6	7:1, 7:2						
8	The Paradox of Theseus's Ship					1:1, 2:6, 2:11		45:3		13:4					
9	Creating a Personal Historical Timeline					1:9, 1:11									
10	Poems Inspired by Art								1:7, 1:10, 9:1, 9:9						
11	Art Inspired by Poetry										3:1, 3:2, 4:1, 4:3				
12	The Paradox of Infinity											1:4, 4:4			
13	Point of View and Cultural Perspectives	2:3, 3:4			1:1, 2:3, 2:4	2:11, 2:14		44:3							

	Activity	Behavior Studies	Civics	Economics	Geography	Historical Understanding	United States History	World History	Language Arts	Science	Visual Arts	Mathematics	Self-Regulation	Music	Thinking & Reasoning
14	The Final Flight of Yamamoto					2:1, 2:4, 2:5	25:2, 25:5	41:3, 41:8							
15	Double Consciousness	1:1, 1:7	14:2, 14:3				20:3, 20:4, 20:5, 31:4, 31:5								
16	The Fable of the Blind Men and the Elephant	1:1, 1:6	27:3, 27:8, 28:1, 28:3						6:1, 6:6, 6:8						
17	Creating a System of Writing								5:2, 6:8						
18	Magic and Technology				9:2, 15:2, 17:2	2:2, 2:6	10:1, 25:4, 26:1	2:1, 4:6, 5:6, 7:4, 35:6, 36:9, 36:14, 40:4		13:1, 13:4					
19	The Birthday Paradox											1:4, 4:4			
20	Möbius Strip and Different Perspectives											1:4, 4:4			
21	Thinking Out of the Paradigm	1:1, 1:2				2:8	2:3, 2:4	26.5							

(Continued)

(Continued)

Activity	Behavior Studies	Civics	Economics	Geography	Historical Understanding	United States History	World History	Language Arts	Science	Visual Arts	Mathematics	Self-Regulation	Music	Thinking & Reasoning
22 Arthur C. Clarke's First Law				9:2, 15:2, 17:2	2:1, 2:2, 2:6	10:1, 25:4, 26:1	2:1, 4:6, 5:6, 7:4, 35:6, 36:9, 36:14, 40:4		13:1, 13:4					
23 Is Technology Neutral?					2:1, 2:2, 2:6		45:3		13:1, 13:4					
24 Writing a Letter to the Editor		25:1, 25:6, 27:3, 27:8						1:4, 1:5, 1:11, 4:2, 4:7, 10:10, 10:12						
25 Science Fiction and Literature as the Future				9:2, 15:2, 17:2	2:1, 2:2, 2:6	10:1, 25:4, 26:1	2:1, 4:6, 5:6, 7:4, 35:6, 36:9, 36:14, 40:4		13:1, 13:4					
26 Creating a Political Broadside		25:1, 25:6, 27:3, 27:8						1:4, 1:5, 1:11, 4:2, 4:7, 10:10, 10:12						
27 Exploring the Great Depression					2:10, 2:11	23:2, 23:3	40:6	8:3						
28 Family Photographs					1:1, 1:2, 2:9, 2:11, 2:12			8:3						

	Activity	Behavior Studies	Civics	Economics	Geography	Historical Understanding	United States History	World History	Language Arts	Science	Visual Arts	Mathematics	Self-Regulation	Music	Thinking & Reasoning
29	Women's Rights						11:1, 12:5, 12:6								
30	Today in History					1:1, 1:2, 2:9, 2:11, 2:12									
31	Photographs of the Farm Security Administration					1:1, 1:2, 2:9, 2:10, 2:11, 2:12	23:2, 23:3				4.3				
32	Primary and Secondary Sources	1:1, 1:3, 1:4				1:1, 1:2, 2:9, 2:11, 2:12									
33	Thinking Outside the Box	1:1, 1:2				2:8									
34	Riddles	1:1, 1:2				2:8									
35	Exploring Community Festivals	1:1, 1:2, 2:2, 2:4			10:1.	2:14									
36	Rebuses and Concrete Writing	1:1, 1:2				2:8			5:2, 5:4, 6:8						
37	Mnemonics	1:1, 1:2				2:8			5:2, 5:4						
38	Designing a Memorial	2:3, 2:4	8:8			2:10, 2:11									
39	Stepping Into a Painting					1:1, 1:2, 2:9, 2:11, 2:12					3:2, 4:1				
40	Japanese Internment During World War II	4:1, 4:3	14:2			2:11, 2:13	25:4	41:3, 41:8	1:9, 8:5, 8:7						

(Continued)

(Continued)

	Activity	Behavior Studies	Civics	Economics	Geography	Historical Understanding	United States History	World History	Language Arts	Science	Visual Arts	Mathematics	Self-Regulation	Music	Thinking & Reasoning
41	ASCII Code														2:8; 2:12; 3:4
42	Protest Songs	4:4	25:1, 25:6, 27:3, 27:8				29:1, 29:4		8:3, 8:9						
43	Inaugural Presidential Address		21:2, 21:3			2:1			8:1, 8:3, 8:9						
44	Portals to the World				13:4, 13:6			44:3, 44:5, 44:6, 44:14							
45	Stories From Childhood					1:1, 1:2, 2:9, 2:11, 2:12			8:3						
46	Round-Robin Stories								2:3, 2:5, 2:7, 8:2, 8:10						
47	Writing Grab Bag								1.1						
48	Using Census Data		15:8		12:4	1:1, 1:2, 2:11			8:5, 8:7						
49	Explore a Favorite Artist								1:10, 2:5, 9:1, 9:2		5:1, 5:2				
50	What Makes a Good Life?								1:6, 1:9				5:7		

	Activity	Behavior Studies	Civics	Economics	Geography	Historical Understanding	United States History	World History	Language Arts	Science	Visual Arts	Mathematics	Self-Regulation	Music	Thinking & Reasoning
51	Creating an Ethical Will					1:1, 1:2, 2:10, 2:11			1:6, 1:11						
52	Written in Stone					1:1, 1:2, 2:10, 2:11									
53	Photographic Timeline					1:1, 1:2, 2:9, 2:11, 2:12			8:3						
54	1900					1:2, 2:10, 2:11	17:4, 17:5, 20:2								
55	95 Theses							27:7							
56	Analyzing *The New England Primer*	1:1, 1:2, 1:3, 1:4, 1:7					4:3, 4:4		5:4, 7:1, 7:4						
57	Slavery in the Constitution?		14:2, 14:3				7:3, 8:1	33:3	5:6, 7:1, 7:4						
58	How Crowded Was the Middle Passage?	4:1, 4:10	14:2, 14:3				3:1								
59	The List					1:1, 1:2, 2:13			4:2, 4:4, 5:4, 7:4						
60	Sacrifices	1:1, 3:3	27:8, 28:1				21:3	39:2, 39:8							

(Continued)

(Continued)

	Activity	Behavior Studies	Civics	Economics	Geography	Historical Understanding	United States History	World History	Language Arts	Science	Visual Arts	Mathematics	Self-Regulation	Music	Thinking & Reasoning
61	The Classroom Missile Crisis	4:1, 4:3					27:4	43:2							
62	Listening to Sources?					2:2, 2:11, 2:12	24:4, 24:5		4:2, 4:3, 4:4					7:2, 7:3	
63	Personal Timelines					1:1; 2:10									
64	Movies as a Window Into History					2:11, 2:12, 2:13	25:5	41:8	9:1, 9:2, 10:1, 10:8, 10:10						
65	Writing Their Own Script					2:11, 2:12			1:6, 1:8, 4:1, 4:6, 4:7						
66	Write Your Own Obituary								1:6, 1:8, 4:2, 4:3						
67	Take a Trip to Mars								1:6, 1:7, 4:2, 4:3	3:5, 13:2, 13:6					
68	CIA Fact Book				13:4, 13:6			44:3, 44:5, 44:6, 44:14	1:6, 1:7, 4:2, 4:3						

	Activity	Behavior Studies	Civics	Economics	Geography	Historical Understanding	United States History	World History	Language Arts	Science	Visual Arts	Mathematics	Self-Regulation	Music	Thinking & Reasoning
69	Talking to an Expert								9:2, 9:3, 9:4, 10:1, 10:2, 10:12		1:2				
70	Famous Last Words								1:6, 1:9, 4:2, 4:3	11:1, 11:3, 11:4, 12:5					
71	Columbus and Culture	2:2, 2:4	1:1, 1:5, 1:7			2:1, 2:5, 2:10									
72	Collage								9:11, 10:2, 10:3		1:1, 1:2, 2:3, 3:2				
73	Making Models								10:3		1:1, 1:2				
74	The World Without Human Life					1:2		46:1	4:2	1:4, 2:6					
75	Creating the Scene for a Story				13:4, 13:6	2:11, 2:12			1:6, 1:8, 4:1, 4:6, 4:7						
76	How Long Is a Thousand Years?					1:1									

(Continued)

(Continued)

	Activity	Behavior Studies	Civics	Economics	Geography	Historical Understanding	United States History	World History	Language Arts	Science	Visual Arts	Mathematics	Self-Regulation	Music	Thinking & Reasoning
77	Creating a Dadaist Poem								6:1, 6:2, 7:5						
78	War Stories	3:3, 3:6	28:3, 28:4			2:10, 2:11			4:3, 4:4						
79	Editorial Cartoons as Social Commentary		11:1, 11:3, 19:6			2:2, 2:12	17:1, 17:4								
80	True or False					2:12, 2:13			4:4, 7:4						1:1, 1:3, 2:2, 2:13
81	Creating Codes											9:7			
82	What Is the Law?		1:3, 1:4, 3:1, 3:2				25:5,	41:3, 41:4	1:6, 1:9						
83	When Is the Law the Law?						7:3, 8:1, 8:3								
84	Symbols in Our Culture	2:3, 2:4				2:5, 2:11		41:4							
85	Symbols on Our Money	2:3, 2:4	9:11			2:5, 2:11									

	Activity	Behavior Studies	Civics	Economics	Geography	Historical Understanding	United States History	World History	Language Arts	Science	Visual Arts	Mathematics	Self-Regulation	Music	Thinking & Reasoning
86	What's on the Stamp?	2:3, 2:4	9:11			2:5, 2:11									
87	Place Names	2:3, 2:4	9:11		4:1, 4:2, 12:5	2:5, 2:11									
88	Art Museums of the World		9:1, 28:4			2:10, 2:13	31:4, 31:5	45:3							
89	America's Attic		9:1, 28:4			2:10, 2:13	31:4, 31:5	45:3							
90	Written in Stone		9:1, 28:4				2:10, 2:13	31:4, 31:5	45:3						
91	Photographic Timeline					1:1, 1:2, 2:9, 2:11, 2:12									
92	The Sounds of Silence								1:5, 1:6, 1:10						
93	What's in a Name?	1:1, 1:3, 1:7, 2:4				2:1									
94	More What's in a Name?	1:1, 1:3, 1:5, 1:6, 1:7, 2:1, 2:2, 2:3, 2:4, 2:5, 4:1				2:1									

(Continued)

(Continued)

	Activity	Behavior Studies	Civics	Economics	Geography	Historical Understanding	United States History	World History	Language Arts	Science	Visual Arts	Mathematics	Self-Regulation	Music	Thinking & Reasoning
95	Crazy Inventions									13:4, 13:5, 13:6					
96	Idioms					1:1			2:1, 2:5, 2:7, 4:1, 4:2, 4:3						
97	Famous Inventions and Their Impact on the World					1:3, 2:2, 2:3, 2:10				11:4, 13:1, 13:2, 13:4, 13:6					
98	What Is in Good Taste?	1:1, 1:6, 3:4									4:1, 4:2, 4:3, 5:1, 5:2, 5:3, 5:4				2:11
99	Creating a Self-Portrait	1:7, 3:3							9:4, 9:8, 9:9, 9:11, 10:6		1:1,1:2, 3:2				
100	Found Art	2:4							9:4, 9:8, 9:9, 9:11, 10:6		3:1, 4:1, 4:2, 4:3, 5:3				

McREL standards available at http://www.mcrel.org/standards-benchmarks/

ACTIVITY 1

Creating a Language

Values	EGYPTIAN			SEMITIC	LATER EQUIVALENTS			
	Hieroglyphic		Hieratic.	Phœnician	Greek.	Roman.	Hebrew	
a	eagle				A	A		1
b	crane				B	B		2
ḳ (g)	throne				Γ	C		3
ṭ (d)	hand				Δ	D		4
h	mæander				E	E		5
f	cerastes				Υ	F		6
z	duck				Ξ	Z		7
χ (kh)	sieve				H	H		8
θ (th)	tongs				Θ	...		9
i	parallels				I	I		10
k	bowl				K	K		11
l	lioness				Λ	L		12
m	owl				M	M		13
n	water				N	N		14
s	chairback				Ξ	X		15
ȧ	....	....	....	......	O	O		16
p	shutter				Π	P		17
t' (ts)	snake				...	...		18
q	angle				...	Q		19
r	mouth				P	R		20
š (sh)	inundated garden				Σ	S		21
t	lasso				T	T		22
	I.	II.	III.	IV.	V.	VI.	VII.	

1

INTRODUCTION

The literary scholar Stanley Fish (2005) has a particularly interesting activity that he does with students in his freshman composition courses. It starts on the first day of class when he gives them the following assignment.

Stanley Fish's Freshman Composition Assignment

You will be divided into groups, and by the end of the semester, each group will be expected to have created its own language, complete with a syntax, a lexicon, a text, rules for translating the text, and strategies for teaching your language to fellow students. The language you create cannot be English or a slightly coded version of English, but it must be capable of indicating the distinctions—between tense, number, mood, agency, and the like—that English enables us to make.

This activity helps students begin to understand the structure of language at its most basic level. All of a sudden it becomes clear that language is not a random mixture of words and phrases; rather, there are very specific rules that govern how language is used. Additionally, it also becomes clear that language represents a cultural creation—one defined and developed by a specific group in a specific way at a specific point in history.

ACTIVITY

Tell students that they will be working in pairs (or groups) to develop a secret language and that they will be assessed by how well their group is able to communicate among themselves solely by using such a language. You might want to give several examples of how different cultures have developed different writing systems, from Sumerian cuneiform to Egyptian hieroglyphics to Chinese *hanzi* to our own Latin alphabet. The key is that there is a logical patterning to the system of symbols that can accommodate distinctions such as color, number, tense, and gender. A symbol could stand for a word (such as in Chinese) or a part of a word (a *phoneme*).

Have students develop the basic code for their language. It may be helpful at intervals to write a short and simple example on the board as a practice round such that students can see if they are making progress. For example, they should be able to write sentences such as these: The man is tall. Two cats were playing. I am hungry. When students feel they have mastered their basic system, have students write notes to each other and decipher each other's writing. An added challenge can be created by having groups switch notes and attempt to decipher each other's codes.

Discuss with students the limitations of their languages, as well as their potential richness. Have students learn the rudiments of another student's language, and then ask them to try to communicate with each other again after their explanations.

ACTIVITY 2

Point-of-View Pictures

INTRODUCTION

How you interpret a political or social issue depends on your point of view. Historians, and other social scientists, know this fact and constantly revise and reinterpret their work. This is often difficult for students to understand. They have a tendency to assume that historical knowledge is absolute and that one can understand things in a fixed and absolute way. The following activity provides an effective way of showing students that by changing one's point of view, or perspective, you can often see things in "new ways."

The preprocess discussion should be based on your specific activity. The key is to explain to your students that what we consider to be truth is oftentimes determined by our position and our perspective. Tell your students that you will now do an activity to make this vivid.

ACTIVITY

Show students the following images one at a time. After looking at each image, have students write a few sentences describing what they think the picture is about. Proceed to each larger part of the photograph.

As students revise their opinions of what the photograph is about, discuss with them how historians revise their interpretations of things as they obtain more information. Analyze how their interpretations can be limited, based on perfectly reasonable assumptions.

(A)

(B)

(C)

(A)   A woman looking at something—possibly a flag
(B)   A woman looking at a policeman in front of what appears to be a bush
(C)   A woman looking at a bride and groom

The photograph is of Paul Phipps and his bride, Nora Langhorne, April 26, 1909. George Grantham Bain photographer. Courtesy of the Library of Congress.

Have students create their own unfolding "point of view" pictures. This may be done through collage, multimedia, or traditional photographs.

ACTIVITY 3

Rosie the Riveter

INTRODUCTION

American women were a significant part of the workforce during World War II. Many successfully worked in heavy industries, where they had previously been excluded because of the assumption that they were too weak to handle the work. Many propaganda posters and photographs such as the ones illustrated in this activity were produced by the Office of War Information. These images portray much about the work women were needed for and their potential role in completing that work. Following the war, many women were pushed out of these jobs as male servicemen returned from serving in the military. The fact that women took over work in so many industries traditionally considered as "male" jobs clearly suggests that our assumptions of what counts as "women's work" and "a man's job" are highly contextual and changing.

A girl mechanic in a large Western aircraft plant rivets the belly of a new consolidated transport plane, 1942. Courtesy of the Library of Congress.

ACTIVITY

Ask students if some jobs are inherently "male" or "female" oriented. Most students may agree that a few jobs—such as being a soldier or firefighter—are gender specific (although even this is far from true). Push students to consider more than these two or three examples. The key is to see whether students assume that some jobs are "naturally" predisposed to certain genders. Explain to the students that at numerous points in history, one gender had to take over all or most of the responsibilities of the other gender. One example is in the former USSR after World War II, where women became the majority of doctors and engineers because so many men died in the war. Another example, closer to home, is the workforce change in the United States during World War II.

Show students the following pictures (or others from the Library of Congress; see the URL on the next page). Have students discuss the meaning of these images. What was their purpose? Who was their audience? Have the students discuss why women gave up these jobs that they evidently did so well.

Extension: Bring in as a guest speaker a woman who worked in the war industries at this time. Use photographs such as the following to discuss with students the role women played in the war effort and American industry.

(A)

(B)

(A) "I've found the job where I fit best!" Find Your War Job In Industry, Agriculture, Business. Washington, D.C.: Office of War Information, 1943. Courtesy of the Library of Congress.

(B) Women welders at the Landers, Frary, and Clark plant; New Britain, Conn. Photographer Gordon Parks, June 1943. Office of War Information. Courtesy of the Library of Congress. Additional images of posters and photographs promoting women in industry during the Second World War can be found online at the American Memory Project of the Library of Congress. Rosie Pictures: Select Images Relating to American Women Workers During World War II. www.loc.gov/rr/print/list/126_rosi.html

Have students discuss to what extent such images and assumptions are dated. To what extent have men and women overcome these definitions and boundaries? Are there analogous pictures and assumptions today?

ACTIVITY 4

Columbus and the Discovery of the New World

INTRODUCTION

The historian Howard Zinn (1980) wrote *A People's History of the United States* from a perspective very different from that of most traditional history books. Rather than focusing on heroic figures such as George Washington or Robert E. Lee, he wrote his work from the viewpoint of those people who had been largely neglected in the history books: indigenous Americans, Black slaves, women, and working people (both native and immigrant). Zinn tried to tell the history of Christopher Columbus's exploration of the New World from the point of view of those who were there when he arrived. Unfortunately, those people left no memories or histories. Zinn turned instead to Columbus's journals, as well as to the journals of Spaniards

who were also on the scene. Zinn's approach is very revealing. Columbus, for example, described the Arawak Indians, or Tainos, as gentle and friendly people: "They do not bear arms. . . . They are the best people in the world and above all the gentlest—without knowledge of what is evil— nor do they murder and steal. . . . They love their neighbors as themselves, and they have the sweetest talk in the world. . . . always laughing" (Zinn, 2005, pp. 98–99). Yet as Zinn points out, despite this analysis on the part of Columbus, the great "Admiral of the Ocean Seas" set in motion a reign of terror on these "gentle and friendly people" during which their lands were taken away from them and they were enslaved in what can accurately be described as a process of social and cultural genocide. As such, one person's "discovery" is very differently viewed from another's perspective.

ACTIVITY

Ask students what it means to discover something. The answers will usually assume that discovery refers to an event with no previous history. For example, one discovers a new path or sees something for the first time. But ask students what would happen if you, the teacher, took one of their pens or a notebook and then claimed that you discovered it. The key is to have students begin to realize that "discovery" involves not just the act but also the later articulation and substantiation of your version of the event.

By using Zinn as a resource or by going back to original documents generated by Columbus and others, a useful classroom discussion and set of critical and reflect activities can be built around Columbus and his "discovery" of the New World. Consider with students the following:

1. Was the "discovery" of the New World a discovery for the indigenous populations or natives of the Western Hemisphere?

2. Is "America," as a name, relevant to the indigenous populations or native populations who were already there?

3. Should indigenous or native populations be compensated for the losses that resulted from the European conquest?

Have students break up into discussion groups to study the meaning of *discovery* and *exploration*. Have them consider the perspectives of those who were conquered and those who conquered. Find out if a defense can be made for conquest and colonization.

Extension: Have students attempt to develop a framework for how a discovery should be claimed. Who should get to decide who discovered what? What happens if two people claim the same discovery?

ACTIVITY 5

How Is History Portrayed? Columbus and the Discovery of the New World

INTRODUCTION

There is no portrait of Christopher Columbus that was painted from life. Yet there are numerous pictures of him and his voyages of discovery. How are such pictures created, and what do they tell us about how history is made? The illustrations included in this activity can be used as a starting point for discussion. Many more portraits of Christopher Columbus and of his voyage to the New World can be found online at the American Memory Project of the Library of Congress (Images of Christopher Columbus and His Voyages are selections from the Collections of the Library of Congress at www.loc.gov/rr/print/list/080_columbus.html).

ACTIVITY

Without preparing your students, announce that you have discovered a new species: *pencil sapiens*. Hold up a pencil. Tell your students that this is a momentous event and that they should all be very proud that they had the opportunity to be a part of this historic occasion. As soon as students question or respond to this claim of the discovery of a new species, tell them to quickly write down a historical account of this discovery for posterity. Explain then to students that much of what we know, or think we know, about historical events is based on journals—and subsequent depictions—much like what they were just writing down. By careful analysis of such journals and depictions, it is possible to understand not only the event but the goal of such journals and depictions.

Show students the following pictures or others from the Library of Congress. Have students analyze the images of Columbus and discovery of the New World. Whose history do the images portray? Have students draw their own pictures of Columbus's voyage and discovery. Have them draw the discovery from the viewpoint of the Arawak Indians who lived on the islands that Columbus discovered. Analyze with them the notion that history is typically written by the people who "won."

(A)

(B)

(C)

(A) Christopher Columbus and his crew leaving the Port of Palos, Spain, for the New World; Crowd of well wishers looks on. Late nineteenth-century color lithograph. Courtesy of the Library of Congress.

(B) First landing of Columbus on the shores of the New World: At San Salvador, W.I., October 12. 1492. New York: Published by Currier & Ives, ca 1892. Courtesy of the Library of Congress.

(C) Christopher Columbus among the Indians. Late nineteenth-century color lithograph. Courtesy of the Library of Congress.

There are numerous analogous examples in current events and issues in Africa, the Middle East, and Asia. Have students choose a specific current event and analyze the situation through an examination of who sets and controls how history gets defined.

ACTIVITY 6

Spanglish

Spanglish: A portmanteau of the words *Spanish* and *English* that refers to the use of English words in Spanish

INTRODUCTION

In the film *Spanglish* (2004), a single Mexican American woman named Flor comes to live in Los Angeles with her young daughter Cristina. Intimidated by American culture, she retreats into the barrio in Los Angeles where she creates a life for herself and her child. Working two jobs to survive, she realizes that as her daughter is getting older, she must spend more time with her. She finds a better paying job with a wealthy couple with two children, but to take the job, she must move into the family's home with her daughter. The movie focuses on the difference between the traditions and assumptions of the Mexican American family and the American family. Food, child rearing, family duty, socioeconomic class, schooling, sexuality, and language are just a few of the issues that become points of friction between the Mexican American woman and her employers. Such differences across and within cultures are becoming more and more common. A key issue is how we as individuals and a culture deal with such differences. One extreme is complete assimilation into another's culture such that the people lose or give up all or most of their past culture and traits. The other extreme is complete segregation from the mainstream culture such that people retain their ways of being in the midst of a completely separate culture. Somewhere in the middle is accommodation to the mainstream culture without complete assimilation or segregation.

Have students watch the film. Ask them to pay attention to how moving, as an individual, across different cultures involves what the educational and cultural theorist Henry Giroux refers to as "border crossing."

ACTIVITY

Have students, working in pairs or groups, construct a list of the differences that Flor encountered. Have students begin to discuss whether and how such differences can be reconciled. Should individuals, for example, have to assimilate into American culture and give up all or most of their own culture? Should this include things such as language, religion, and food? Have students develop an argument for where the line is between assimilation and segregation to a mainstream culture and if this line changes due to specific issues.

Extension: For a contrast with this film, have students watch the 1983 film *El Norte,* in which another Latino maid comes to work in an Anglo household. One of the classic scenes involves the main character finding the washer-dryer so baffling that she simply spreads the laundry on the lawn to dry in the sun. Have students compare and contrast these two films and perhaps analyze what being an "alien" actually means.

ACTIVITY 7

Slave Narratives

Slave Narratives from the Federal Writers' Project, 1936-1938

INTRODUCTION

Among the most remarkable collections found online at the Library of Congress are the slave narratives from the Federal Writers' Project. The collection includes more than 2,300 first-person accounts of slavery and 500 black-and-white photographs of former slaves. The interviews were compiled during the Great Depression of the 1930s as part of the Federal Writers' Project of the Works Progress Administration (WPA). They are available as texts online at the address found below. In addition, photographs of many of the interviewees are available, as well as actual audio files of their interviews.

ACTIVITY

Begin a discussion about how slavery seems like such a distant event. And while it in fact did occur a long time ago, many of the people who were slaves lived up to the time that the students' parents were young. Explain to them that the Library of Congress has a huge collection of interviews and photographs of individuals who lived through slavery. See Born in Slavery at http://memory.loc.gov/ammem/snhtml/snhome.html.

Have students access the Library of Congress Web site. These interviews can be used in many ways by students. Consider the following possibilities:

1. Have a student review a former slave interview and become expert on it. Activities could include having students present the former slave as part of an oral presentation in class, writing a report or profile on them that could be posted online or on a class bulletin board.
2. Have students work in groups to review interviews and pull common themes out of the interviews (treatment by owners, education under slavery, etc.).
3. If students live in one of the areas where the interviews were conducted, see if they can find relatives of the former slaves who still live in the community. Have them discuss with these individuals their experience as African Americans living in the United States. (It may be possible that a student is related to someone who was interviewed.)

Discuss with students how this archive has saved a critical aspect of this country's history.

Extension: Brainstorm what events in your school or local community may also be important to archive for future students or generations. Consider developing an archival project that documents the chosen event or issue.

ACTIVITY 8

The Paradox of Theseus's Ship

INTRODUCTION

Theseus is the hero in Greek mythology who felled the Minotaur, a half-man, half-bull monster who lived in the labyrinth on the island of Crete. According to the Roman historian Plutarch, the ship that Theseus sailed on back to Athens from Crete was preserved over hundreds of years. Its old and worn-out planks were replaced by new ones as they became too old. Supposedly so much work was done on the ship that nothing of the original remained. The question eventually arose: Was this still Theseus's ship?

ACTIVITY

Make a copy of a dollar bill and pass it around. Ask students if this copy is as good as the original. Since most students will say "no," introduce the myth of Theseus. Explain that in our society almost everything is a copy of an original mold (this includes the desks in the classroom, the pens they are using, the cars they came to school in, etc.).

Have students discuss what is real and what is a copy. Give them an assignment where they must find a copy of a real thing, and then have them defend it as being as good as the original. Have them find an original example of something and then have them make a case for why it is superior to a copy or simulation.

Have students write a short paper arguing one perspective (that a copy is or is not as good as an original).

Develop a student discussion that has them consider whether or not a cast sculpture becomes less valuable as more and more copies are made. Is Rodin's bronze sculpture *The Thinker* the same if it is reproduced from the same mold only once or a hundred times?

ACTIVITY 9

Creating a Personal Historical Timeline

INTRODUCTION

Having students relate to recent historical events can be difficult. History—even recent history—often seems distant and abstract. A way to overcome this problem is by having students create their own personal historical timelines. Personal historical timelines should start on the day or year when a student was born. They can include not only political events but information about how much things cost compared with today, new movies, and disasters such as floods or hurricanes. Students can obtain information from local and national newspapers, magazines, almanacs, and general histories. A wide range of historical timelines can be found at various sites on the Internet. Personal photographs can be integrated into the timeline as well as historical photographs.

ACTIVITY

Explain to students that history is not something far away and long ago. Every day has relevance. Explain to students that they will discover how important dates in their own lives (such as one's birthday) can be linked to many other important dates. Pass out the Model Timeline Worksheet.

Provide students with the following helpful Internet resources:

1. This site provides a list of famous people born on each day of the year: www.born-today.com

2. This site provides a listing of famous events on any day in the year: www.historychanel.com/today

3. Alterna Time is an excellent Web site that provides links to dozens of sites on the Internet that have timelines: www2.canisius.edu/~emeryg/time.html

In addition, using the Google search engine, type in "today in history." You will find numerous links to Web sites that deal with historical events on specific days in history.

This activity can become intergenerational by having students create timelines for older members of their family, including parents and grandparents. Students can make timelines for others in their family or for their friends.

Model Timeline

<<My Name>> Personal Timeline	International Events
I was born on April 23, 1963	William Shakespeare was born the same day in 1564.

ACTIVITY 10

Poems Inspired by Art[1]

Pieter Brueghel, *The Fall of Icarus*; Oil-tempera, 29 inches × 44 inches; Museum of Fine Arts, Brussels.

INTRODUCTION

Many poems have been inspired by works of art. One of the most interesting is by the American poet William Carlos Williams (1883–1963). It is called "Landscape With the Fall of Icarus" and is based on a painting by the Dutch painter Pieter Brueghel the Elder (1525–1569) titled *The Fall of Icarus*. Interestingly, Brueghel's depiction is highly understated given the riveting Greek myth of Icarus's fall.

"Landscape With the Fall of Icarus"
William Carlos Williams

According to Brueghel
when Icarus fell
it was spring

a farmer was ploughing
his field
the whole pageantry

of the year was
awake tingling
near

the edge of the sea
concerned
with itself

sweating in the sun
that melted
the wings' wax

unsignificantly
off the coast
there was

a splash quite unnoticed
this was
Icarus drowning

ACTIVITY

Have students (in groups or pairs) read the poem and compare it with the painting. Have them discuss or write about these questions: Why did William Carlos Williams focus on certain parts of the painting and not others? What did Williams leave out? Why do you think he did that?

Have students choose a favorite work of art and use it as the basis for creating a poem or story of their own.

Some other famous poems based on paintings or other works of art include the following:

1. "The Walking Man of Rodin" by Carl Sandburg

2. "Monet's *Waterlilies*" by Robert Hayden

3. "The Starry Night" by Anne Sexton

4. "Ode on a Grecian Urn" by John Keats

Extension (or preprocess): Have students read the original Greek myth (see http://etext .virginia.edu/latin/ovid/trans/Ovhome.htm#askline) and then compare the myth with both the painting and the poem. The key here is to note how much the story changes and gains newfound significance from different artists/writers and why these changes may be of significance. An interesting example of the story can be found at the University of Virginia's Electronic Text Center. The story is found in Bk VIII:183-235 Daedalus and Icarus.

Note

1. This activity is based on an idea by Brenda Loreman, Arroyo High School, San Lorenzo, California.

ACTIVITY 11

Art Inspired by Poetry

INTRODUCTION

Among the most interesting poems to inspire a famous painting is William Carlos Williams's (1883–1963) "The Great Figure." This poem inspired Charles Demuth's (1883–1935) painting *The Figure 5 in Gold*.

"The Great Figure"
William Carlos Williams

Among the rain
and lights
I saw the figure 5
in gold
on a red
firetruck
moving
tense
unheeded
to gong clangs
siren howls
and wheels rumbling
through the dark city.

Source: Collected Poems: 1909–1939, Vol. I, © 1938 by William Carlos Williams, p. 174. Reprinted by permission of New Directions Publishing Corp.

ACTIVITY

Show students an illustration of the painting, which is included in the collection of the Metropolitan Museum of Art. You can find an illustration oƒ the painting at the museum's Web site: www.metmuseum.org/toah/ho/11/na/hod_49.59.1.htm. Another useful Web site with information on the painting is www.wisdomportal.com/Christmas/Figure5InGold.html.

Have them write a paragraph explaining what they think the painting is about. Then have them read the poem by the American poet William Carlos Williams (1883–1963), which was the inspiration for the painting.

Have students choose a favorite painting or other work of art and use it to create a poem of their own. Have them present their poems in class along with the artworks that inspired them. Assess the poems produced based on how carefully and creatively they followed the chosen painting.

Help students create an anthology of the poems and artworks, or display them online or on a bulletin board.

ACTIVITY 12

The Paradox of Infinity

INTRODUCTION

Zeno of Elea (ca 450 BCE) is famous for creating a number of paradoxes, including "Theseus's Ship" (Activity 8), "The Tortoise and Achilles," and "The Paradox of the Arrow in Flight." According to "Zeno's Paradox of the Tortoise and Achilles," the tortoise challenged Achilles, the hero of the *Iliad*, to a race. The tortoise claimed that he could win the race as long as Achilles gave him a small advantage. The original description of the story is somewhat confusing, but basically what Zeno proposes is the following paradox:

Zeno's Paradox of the Tortoise and Achilles

Suppose you wish to cross a room. First, go half the distance, then another half, and so on until you reach the other side. How long will it take you to reach the opposite end of the room?

The answer is never.

ACTIVITY

Have students actually try to measure out a room as described in this paradox. Lead them, step-by-step, in going halfway across the room, then half again, and so on.

Have students form groups to discuss whether they would have ever reached the end of the room and how this relates to the concept of infinity.

This activity neatly demonstrates the main aspect of a paradox: It provides two seemingly contradictory events that nevertheless are seemingly combined—a bounded distance (the length of the room) and an unbounded length of time (the infinite number of steps). Use this activity to examine how paradoxes function and what other paradoxes the students can come up with.

Discuss with students Zeno's "Paradox of the Arrow in Flight," which asks where is an arrow if it is in flight. Discuss why this might be an important idea in terms of understanding physics. Can an object, for example, be somewhere if it is in motion?

ACTIVITY 13

Point of View and Cultural Perspectives

INTRODUCTION

Gerhardus Mercator (1512–1594) is the Latin name for the Flemish geographer, mathematician, and cartographer Gerhard Kremer. Mercator is most well known for creating the type of map known as a Mercator projection. In a Mercator projection, the parallels of latitude, which on the globe are equal distances apart, are drawn with increasing separation as the areas being mapped move closer to either the North or South Pole. Mercator's approach makes it possible to take a round planet (the Earth) and map it on a flat surface (paper). However, using this process creates some problems, since areas mapped are exaggerated as they get more and more distant from the equator. Thus, the size of Greenland and Antarctica are exaggerated in a Mercator projection, while preserving their actual shape. As a result, Mercator projections give an incorrect idea of the relative size of different land masses in which those closer to the North or South Pole seem larger than those closest to the Equator.

On a Mercator projection, Greenland looks larger than China, Europe, or South America, when in fact it is smaller (0.8 square million miles versus 3.7 million miles for China, 3.8 square million miles for Europe, and 6.9 square million miles for South America).

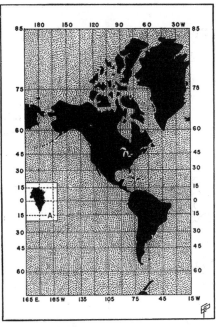

ACTIVITY

Have students discuss how the Mercator projection may distort our understanding of the world. Ask them why Mercator projection maps of the world always have their center in Europe?

Have students draw a detailed map of their town. Have them bring their maps to class and post them on a bulletin board. Then have them analyze in the form of a class discussion or an essay the characteristics of their maps. What do they emphasize? What do they ignore? Discuss with them how the maps they have made are cultural constructions with their own points of view and potential biases.

ACTIVITY 14

Final Flight of Yamamoto: Should We Have Struck Back?

Admiral Isoroku Yamamoto (1884–1943).

INTRODUCTION

Admiral Isoroku Yamamoto (1884–1943) was a military strategist of the highest order. He pioneered naval aviation in the Japanese fleet, functioning as a crucial supporter of increased training for naval aviators and a major proponent for the construction of a revolutionary new vessel: floating airports known as aircraft carriers. Yamamoto was also a scholar, having studied at the postgraduate level in the United States. He traveled throughout the country and later served as a naval attaché in Washington, D.C. At the opening of hostilities in the Pacific during the 1930s, Yamamoto made it clear to his superiors in the military and the government that he did not believe Japan could defeat America and its allies in the West.

Yet when conflict did arise between the United States and Japan, Admiral Yamamoto played a central role in the opening acts of the drama. As Commander-in-Chief of the Combined Fleet, the crown jewel of the Imperial military, Yamamoto was the operational chieftain of the entire Japanese fleet. Serving in this role, he planned the surprise attack against Pearl Harbor, though he planned for the United States to be delivered a declaration of hostilities just moments before the attack began. Throughout the first few years of World War II, Yamamoto was the strategic mastermind in the navy's successful campaign of conquest in the South Pacific and in the opening sea fights with the U.S. Navy. Then, in April of 1943, Admiral Yamamoto was removed from the war and placed into the history books.

Using decoded Japanese missives, the United States discovered that Yamamoto would be visiting a forward base in an attempt to boost the morale of his frontline troops. The code breakers in the Pentagon were able to tell army planners the exact details of Yamamoto's flight. With this information in hand, Admiral Nimitz and the Roosevelt administration gave the green light to an attack by the Army Air Force on Admiral Yamamoto's flight. The American pilots, armed with such detailed intelligence, were successful in shooting the Admiral's plane down into the forests of Rabaul, New Guinea. The fate of Admiral Yamamoto is an excellent opportunity to introduce students to the debate surrounding targeting of individuals who are deemed a threat to the United States. Despite having occurred in wartime, many historians have categorized Yamamoto's death as nothing short of an assassination.

ACTIVITY

Divide students into groups or teams and instruct different groupings to argue for or against the U.S. decision to kill Yamamoto.

Encourage students to consider Yamamoto's earlier opposition to the war and his unique appreciation for the West's capabilities. What if Yamamoto might have been a figure capable of bringing an earlier conclusion to the Pacific War? Would the United States still have been responsible in seeking revenge (justice) for the attack on Pearl Harbor?

In a modern era of cruise missiles and satellite imagery, governments have a new ability to aim unexpected attacks at a single individual as never before. Discuss with students if the use of such methods has serious problems attached to it or if its use is justified.

ACTIVITY 15

Double Consciousness: Examining Oneself and the Concept of Privilege

"Am I Not a Man and a Brother?" This engraving of a slave in chains was published in 1835 as the header for a broadside on which appeared John Greenleaf Whittier's poem "My Countrymen in Chains!" The illustration and the motto date back to the abolitionist movement in eighteenth-century England. In 1787, the Quaker-led Society for Effecting the Abolition of the Slave Trade met in London, and a committee was charged with preparing the design for a seal. Later that year, the design and motto were approved by the society. Josiah Wedgwood, the pottery manufacturer who was a member of the society, manufactured a jasperware cameo/medallion of the image. In 1788, a shipment of the cameos was sent to Benjamin Franklin in Philadelphia. The image was published in many different versions prior to the Civil War. Courtesy of the Library of Congress.

INTRODUCTION

In Chapter 1 of *The Souls of Black Folk*, W. E. B. Du Bois (1907) introduces the concept of "double consciousness,"[1] explaining,

After the Egyptian and Indian, the Greek and Roman, the Teuton and Mongolian, the Negro is a sort of seventh son,[2] born with a veil, and gifted with second-sight in this American world,—a world which yields him no true self-consciousness, but only lets him see himself through the revelation of the other world. It is a peculiar sensation, this double consciousness, this sense of always looking at one's self through the eyes of others, of measuring one's soul by the tape of a world that looks on in amused contempt and pity. One ever feels his twoness,—an American, a Negro; two souls, two thoughts, two unreconciled strivings; two warring ideals in one dark body, whose dogged strength alone keeps it from being torn asunder. (p. 3)

Du Bois's use of the concept of "double consciousness" is among the most important from his work. It is also an important concept for those interested in African American studies and American history. It can be used as an interesting means by which to examine one's own understanding of self as well as the concept of privilege in American society.

ACTIVITY

In this activity you will look at privilege and how it works based on where you are situated, socially and culturally. This activity requires you to assume a series of *different* identities and then examine how your life might be different or the same.

As an assignment that can raise very deep questions and stir serious personal thoughts, this activity is best suited for individual work. As such, the following mostly self-explanatory hand-out can be used as the basis for this individual work.

Double Consciousness: Examining Oneself and the Concept of Privilege

If you are a man, for example, imagine that you are a woman. If you are rich or moderately well-to-do economically, imagine that you are poor. If you are poor, imagine being moderately well-to-do or very rich. Consider other perspectives, such as being the member of a different race or of a different sexual orientation. How would they change your life?

Are there certain privileges you feel that you would gain or lose if you were to "reverse" who and what you are? List what you think you would gain or lose below.

Gender:

Socioeconomic level:

Race:

Sexual orientation:

Imagine yourself as your *second* or *other* self. Write an essay describing what you think your life and experience would be if you found yourself different from who and what you are. If you like, extend your analysis by imagining what privileges you would gain or lose by being an athlete or not being an athlete, by being a musician or not being a musician, and so on.

Notes

1. The idea of "double consciousness" is among the most important ideas developed by Du Bois in *The Souls of Black Folks*. Its significance is analyzed in detail in Dickson D. Bruce, Jr.'s (1992) "W. E. B. Du Bois and the Idea of Double Consciousness."

2. In Black folklore, seventh sons are believed to have supernatural powers, including the ability to see the future and to perceive individuals from the spirit world.

ACTIVITY 16

The Fable of the Blind Men and the Elephant

INTRODUCTION

The American John Godfrey Saxe (1816–1887) is most famous for his poem based on the Indian fable of the blind men and the elephant, where six blind men feel different parts of an elephant and try to describe what the animal is like. The fable and poem provide a powerful metaphor for students to understand the limitations of their own point of view or perspective on the world.

"The Blind Men and the Elephant"
John G. Saxe

It was six men of Indostan,
To learning much inclined,
Who went to see the elephant,
(Though all of them were blind,)
That each by observation
Might satisfy his mind.

The first approached the elephant,
And, happening to fall
Against his broad and sturdy side,
At once began to bawl
"God bless me! but the elephant
Is very like a wall!"

The second, feeling of the tusk,
Cried: "Ho! what have we here.
So very round, and smooth, and sharp?
To me 'tis very clear,
This wonder of an elephant
Is very like a spear!"

The third approached the animal,
And, happening to take
The squirming trunk within his hands,
Thus boldly up he spoke:
"I see," quoth he, "the elephant
Is very like a snake!"

The fourth reached out his eager hand,
And felt about the knee:
"What most this wondrous beast is like
Is very plain," quoth he;
"'Tis clear enough the elephant
Is very like a tree!"

The fifth, who chanced to touch the ear,
Said: "E'en the blindest man
Can tell what this resembles most:
Deny the fact who can,
This marvel of an elephant
Is very like a fan!"

The sixth no sooner had begun
About the beast to grope,
Than, seizing on the swinging tail
That fell within his scope,
"I see," quoth he, "the elephant
Is very like a rope!"

And so these men of Indostan
Disputed loud and long,
Each in his own opinion
Exceeding stiff and strong,
Though each was partly in the right
And all were in the wrong!

"The Blind Men and the Elephant," *The Poems of John Godfrey Saxe,* by John Godfrey Saxe. Boston: James R. Osgood, 1873, p. 135.

ACTIVITY

Have students compile a list of the things that influence how they see the world. These could include religion, geography, social class, ethnic background, race, gender, and so on. Discuss with them how the way they see the world also has the potential to make them blind to certain things. In particular, have them think about how they might view certain issues if they came from different backgrounds and experiences.

Explore critically a political or social issue. Should the United States be engaged in wars overseas? Should taxes be the same for all people? Should people be allowed to commit suicide with the assistance of a physician? Have students consider how their values and experiences allow them to "see what the elephant really is" or how what they see is obscured.

ACTIVITY 17

Creating a System of Writing

INTRODUCTION

Literacy is defined as the ability to read and write. We take its order and forms largely for granted. To do so is to fail to realize that how we write determines how we read. In modern English, we use a phonetic alphabet. How does this influence the process of learning how to read? Think about a logographic- or symbol-based system of writing such as Chinese or Japanese. How is this process of learning to read and write different from a phonetic system such as English or French?

ACTIVITY

Have students create a logographic (symbolic or pictorial) writing system for English. In doing so, have them try to think about the advantages and disadvantages of such a writing system over our present system of an alphabetically/phonetically based writing style.

Have students write the five following sentences in their invented system:

1. The doe jumped over the wooden fence.
2. I love you.
3. Look at the sunset.
4. Power is knowledge.
5. My name is <fill in your name>.

Have students consider these questions:

1. How do the technologies of writing potentially affect the effectiveness and ease of their system of writing?
2. What if the only tools were styluses and clay tablets? (Sumerian)
3. Or styluses and wax tables? (Roman)
4. Or sheepskin and quill? (medieval)
5. Or quill and paper? (late medieval and Renaissance)

Consider how publishing in a logographic system such as Chinese is different from publishing in English. How is the type that is used different? How does a typewriter used in English compare with a typewriter used in Chinese? How does the composition of text documents change in Chinese or Japanese with the introduction of computers and inkjet printers? Have students consider why calligraphy is an important element of Chinese and Japanese art and culture and why it is not as important in Western art and culture.

ACTIVITY 18

Magic and Technology

Any sufficiently advanced technology is indistinguishable from magic.

—Arthur C. Clarke, 1984

INTRODUCTION

During the Renaissance and early modern period, scientists such as Paracelsus (1493–1541) and Isaac Newton (1643–1727) also experimented with magic and alchemy (a pseudoscientific forerunner of chemistry). Often, scientific discoveries have appeared to be little different from magic.

ACTIVITY

Turn the lights on and off. Tell students that you have just done something magical. When they disagree, argue that since they can't explain how you did it, then it must be magic. Focus the class on how many new technologies, by being nonobvious at the time, appeared as if they were magic.

Have students compile a list of five scientific and technological discoveries that would appear to be magic to someone who lived two hundred years ago. Give a hint to students; for example, what would television have appeared to be to someone such as George Washington or Thomas Jefferson?

Discuss with students what distinguishes science from magic. Explore with them what is a science and what is a pseudoscience. For example, compare the difference between astrology and astronomy. Have students look up definitions of each on the Internet or in a good encyclopedia. Distinguish how one (astronomy) is a science and one (astrology) is a pseudoscience.

Have students develop an argument for how to tell the difference between science and pseudoscience.

ACTIVITY 19

The Birthday Paradox

INTRODUCTION

A paradox is what appears to be a true statement or set of statements that leads to a contradiction to what seems like an intuitively correct answer. Often, paradoxes lead to significant advances in science, philosophy, and mathematics by pointing to new ways of looking at things or to limitations in how our view of the world is constructed.

One of the most interesting of all paradoxes is the "birthday paradox." According to the paradox, which is based on theories of probability, if there are 23 or more people in a room, then there is a chance of more than 50 percent that at least two of them will have the same birthday. For 60 or more people, the probability is already greater than 99 percent that someone will have the same birthday.

The birthday paradox is not a paradox in the sense of its leading to logical contradiction. Instead, it is a paradox in that it is counterintuitive. To understand the birthday paradox, it is necessary to understand that there are many possible pairs of people whose birthdays could match. With 23 people, there are C(23,2) = 23 × 22/2 = 253 pairs, with a potential candidate for a match.

ACTIVITY

Ask students to go up to the board and write down their birthdays. If you have a small class, it may be possible (and helpful) to ask a class next door to take a minute to come in and write birthdays down as well. The likelihood is that two students will have the same birthday. Discuss the seeming amazing aspect of this "coincidence" given that there are 365 days in the year.

Using the mathematical formula above, have students determine what would be the likelihood of 10 people in a room having the same birthday. Have them consider 50, 100, 200, and 300. Ask students how understanding probability could give them an advantage in making a bet. Ask them how knowledge of probability works to the advantage of people who own casinos and other venues for legalized gambling.

A variation on the birthday paradox is the idea of "six degrees of separation." In fact, a recent Hollywood movie, *Six Degrees of Separation*, is based on the principle, which states that there are only six individuals who separate you from almost anyone in the world. That seems amazing until you know about geometric proportions. If you know 500 people, and each of them knows 500 people, and they each know 500 people, then there would be a network created of 125 million people. Although there would be doubling in many instances, the numbers would be nonetheless enormous.

Extension: Have students research on the Internet the idea of six degrees of separation and the concept known as "six degrees of Kevin Bacon," which suggests that everyone in Hollywood is somehow connected fairly closely to the actor Kevin Bacon.

ACTIVITY 20

Möbius Strip and Different Perspectives

INTRODUCTION

A Möbius strip is a one-sided surface that can be constructed by affixing the ends of a rectangular strip after first having given one of the ends a one-half twist. This space exhibits interesting properties, such as having only one side and remaining in one piece when split down the middle. Its properties were discovered independently by two German mathematicians, August Ferdinand Möbius and Johann Benedict Listing, in 1858.

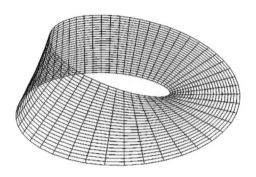

ACTIVITY

Prepare kits for each student in your class. The kits must include a handout with instructions (see the following sample handout) and one to three strips of paper about five to six inches in length. The extra strips are just in case some students require more than one attempt.

Instead of printing out multiple copies, another option would be simply to write the instructions on a classroom board before the class enters or to prepare an overhead projection.

Möbius Strip and Different Perspectives

You can create a Möbius strip using the following steps.

1. Take a strip of paper five or six inches in length.

2. Give it a half twist (turn one end over).

3. After you make your Möbius strip, take a pencil and draw a line along the length. How many sides does the Möbius strip have?

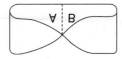

It may also be helpful to prepare a demonstration Möbius strip to use yourself. This strip should be larger than the standard student strip in order to be better employed as a visual aid.

Take a pair of scissors and cut the Möbius strip along the line you have drawn. What happens?

Möbius strips are often used as belts in machinery because they last longer. Why is this the case? Discuss with students where is the top and where is the bottom of a Möbius strip. Discuss with students how the physical universe does not always fit our preconceptions.

Have students design a space station using a Möbius strip. Have them be as innovative as possible. What would be some of the advantages of such a design compared with a more traditional round space station?

ACTIVITY 21

Thinking Out of the Paradigm: The Columbus Egg Problem

INTRODUCTION

According to legend, Christopher Columbus (1451–1506) was having dinner with a group of Spanish gentlemen. A rather proud and conceited lot, they said to him that his discovery of new lands across the Atlantic Ocean wasn't that much of an accomplishment. In fact, discovering them was the simplest thing in the world.

Columbus at first did not make any reply. After a bit though, he took an egg from a dish on the table and asked, "Who can make this egg stand on end?" Each of the men tried. None of them was successful. All of them said it was impossible for the egg to stand upright on its own.

Finally, Columbus took the egg and gently crushed its bottom, allowing it to stand upright. He then said, "What you said is impossible is the simplest thing to accomplish when you have the answer."

What Columbus did was break the existing paradigm. A paradigm is a way of looking at or interpreting the world. This is sometimes referred to as "thinking outside the box."

ACTIVITY

You can present the Columbus egg problem to your students. Bring a hard-boiled egg to class and pose the problem to them. We don't know if Columbus's egg was hard-boiled, but it is a lot less messy than using a raw one! Suggest that they use whatever means they like to have the egg stand upright on its own but emphasize that they solve the problem in the most simple and elegant way possible. Show them the solution using the hard-boiled egg, which you can eat after class as a snack!

Students may argue that the solution to the problem is "cheating." Explore whether or not a creative solution to a problem that goes outside traditional methods is legitimate. Have them examine how many of our greatest explorers, inventors, and artists have often broken with tradition.

Have students develop their own "outside the box" activity and demonstrate it to the class or to their group.

ACTIVITY 22

Arthur C. Clarke's First Law

When a distinguished but elderly scientist states that something is possible, he is almost certainly right. When he states that something is impossible, he is very probably wrong.

—Arthur C. Clarke, 1984

INTRODUCTION

Clarke has also predicted that we will eventually drop superstrong diamond filaments from satellites in geosynchronous orbits (a distance of roughly 20,000 miles). Because of the rotation of the earth, these space elevators or railways would have to be at the equator. NASA is seriously studying the possibility of such structures using nanotechnology (a type of engineering devoted to the design and production of extremely small objects built from individual atoms and molecules). Is such an idea absurd?

ACTIVITY

Have students list five things that exist in the modern world that people would have considered impossible two hundred years ago. Have them discuss the consequences of new inventions and discoveries that may develop in the future. What would happen if it becomes possible to extend people's lives another twenty-five or fifty years? The life expectancy of most people was approximately fifty years in 1900; today it is close to eighty years. What types of things would be affected? Social relations? Health care? Economics?

Many people think it will be possible in the next twenty-five to fifty years to copy a human consciousness and store it in a computer. If this happens, will the consciousness in the computer be alive? If someone turns off the computer and its memory is erased, will this be the same as murder? Can a computer consciousness potentially commit murder or slander? Can it be legally liable? Have students write a one-page scenario outlining some of the ethical, social, and moral implications that would exist if such a thing came to pass.

ACTIVITY 23

Is Technology Neutral?

INTRODUCTION

Technologies surround us in our modern lives to such a degree that their use becomes largely invisible and taken for granted.

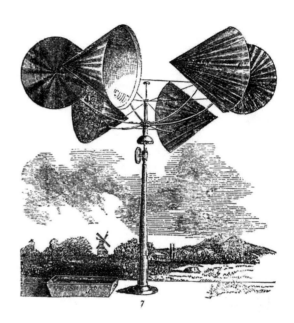

Think for a moment about how your life would be different without certain technologies. For example, imagine what the world would be like without automobiles. How might the city or town where you live be different? Where would people work, live, play? How would the lack of cars affect architecture? Would social activities change?

The German philosopher Martin Heidegger (1889–1976) argued that technologies have the potential to enhance and diminish (magnify and limit) certain aspects of our lives. Think about the technology of the cell phone. What does it enhance and diminish? What types of issues are involved in determining the use of this technology?

ACTIVITY

Make a list of all the technologies you encounter in your day-to-day life. List every technology you used yesterday. Include things such as alarm clocks, toothbrushes, automobiles, electric lights, and so on. How many of these technologies could you give up easily? How many are essential to your life? How do the technologies you use affect your social and personal interactions with other people?

ACTIVITY 24

Writing a Letter to the Editor

INTRODUCTION

There is a long tradition of writing letters to the editor in newspapers and magazines. It has been a way to make one's voice heard and to be part of a larger public conversation.

ACTIVITY

Have students choose an issue or topic at a local level that is of interest to them. For example, in Staunton, Virginia, there is a debate over whether or not the local state school for the deaf and blind should be closed and replaced with a more modern campus elsewhere in the region. The school, which has existed since the Civil War, has been an integral part of the community. Its removal would cause the loss of many jobs as well as require the replacement of expensive buildings. On the other hand, there is the argument that the school is inconveniently located for many of the students who attend it, that the buildings need to be updated, and that the campus doesn't look modern.

Have students research an issue they care about, and then have them construct a carefully written letter outlining their opinion. Have students use letters to the editor in various magazines and newspapers as models. Discuss with them the need to be clear about their opinions. Make sure that no letter runs more than three or four paragraphs. Emphasize the idea that "less may be more."

In class, have students create a list of topics that are of interest to them and that are discussed in the local newspaper. For example, Should stem cell research be allowed? Should we have a flat tax for the entire population? As a class, choose a common issue for them to research and find out more about.

Next, have students find at least three newspaper articles that discuss the issues surrounding the topic chosen for discussion. Have them copy these articles and summarize the key points for each.

Develop a classroom discussion in which students present their findings. Have them compile notes as the discussion takes place. From these notes, and based on their own research, have them write a position paper on the issue, one to two pages in length.

Consider sending the letters to the local newspaper or publishing them in the school's newspaper.

ACTIVITY 25

Science Fiction and Literature as the Future

Politicians should read science fiction, not westerns and detective stories.

—Arthur C. Clarke, 1984

INTRODUCTION

Science fiction often anticipates what happens only a few years later. Jules Verne (1828–1905) predicted men visiting the polar caps in submarines and the moon in a rocket. What looks very much like a nuclear submarine appears in his novel *Twenty Thousand Leagues Under the Sea* (1870).

Aldous Huxley in his 1932 novel *Brave New World* predicted that cloning—the process of making genetically identical copies—would be possible in the future, something that has indeed been realized in recent years.

ACTIVITY

Have students watch a part of the science fiction movie such as *Blade Runner* (1982) or show a portion of an episode from the original *Star Trek* television series (1966–1969). Discuss what aspects of the technology have come into existence, what has not, and what might still be developed.

Encourage students to look at different science fiction stories and films and have them consider whether or not what they predict is likely to become a reality. Have them write a short story or the treatment for a film based on technologies that do not yet exist. The movie *Minority Report* (2002), for example, suggested that in the future, police would be able to read the minds of people to determine if a crime would occur *before the criminal even committed the crime*. Is this possible? Is it ethical?

Have students choose a seemingly unrealistic scenario (such as living forever or cloning oneself) and create a movie idea based on this scenario and the consequences of such a scenario actually coming to be.

ACTIVITY 26

Creating a Political Broadside

INTRODUCTION

In the Colonial era, one of the main ways to get out a political message was to write and print a broadside. Broadsides are single sheets of paper on which political messages are printed on one side. Typically, broadsides were printed in large numbers and distributed for free, usually tacked up in town squares, taverns, and churches. Broadsides could announce a government decision, discuss a political issue, or announce a literary or artistic event.

In the nineteenth century, broadsides were used widely in politics. Perhaps the most famous broadside from the nineteenth century shows the division of Essex County, Massachusetts, in 1812 so as to benefit the Jeffersonian Republicans in an upcoming senatorial election. Elbridge Gerry, the state's governor, reluctantly signed the redistricting law. Opponents created a broadside titled "The Gerry-mander: a new species of monster, which appeared in Essex South District in Jan. 1812." The illustration accompanying the text shows a salamander-type monster in the shape of the redrawn voting district. The term *gerrymander* is an eponym— a word based on someone's name. In this, case Governor Gerry.

You can learn more about broadsides by visiting the Library of Congress American Memory Project Web site (http://memory.loc.gov/ammem/rbpehtml/pehome.html), "An American Time Capsule: Three Centuries of Broadsides and Other Printed Ephemera," which contains hundreds of different examples of American broadsides and pamphlets.

ACTIVITY

Visit the Library of Congress Web site on broadsides and get ideas from it to create your own broadside. Design your broadside so it fits on one side of an 8.5 × 11-inch sheet of paper. Make sure that it includes both an illustration and detailed text (at least two or three paragraphs in length). Your broadside can be based on a social or political issue, or it can announce a literary or artistic event. It should be much more than just a flyer.

As an additional activity, have students explore political and social blogs online.

ACTIVITY 27

Exploring the Great Depression

INTRODUCTION

The Great Depression in the United States began with the crash of the stock market in October of 1929 and continued for a decade until the late 1930s. It was the most severe depression of modern history. For many people, it was a life-changing event.

ACTIVITY

Have students talk to their grandparents and great-grandparents or older members of the community about

Migratory packinghouse workers waiting around post office during slack season. Belle Grande, Florida. Photograph by Marion Post Wolcott, 1939. Courtesy of the Library of Congress.

the Great Depression. Make sure they talk with someone old enough to have lived during the Depression and who can remember it. He or she will have to be at least 72 years old.

Before conducting their interviews, have students collect sources of information about the Depression. Appropriate sections of textbooks, as well as library resources, can be drawn on. Sources can be found beyond traditional histories, such as John Steinbeck's *The Grapes of Wrath* or the John Ford movie based on the book.

If at all possible, have students tape-record or videotape their interviews. Make sure they label their interviews with the date, time, and place of the interview. Have students run a voice-level check before they begin their interview, and be sure that they introduce the person they are interviewing, spelling out his or her name, the date and place of the interview, the interviewer, and the name of the interviewer at the beginning of the tape.

If students are not recording their interview but, rather, taking notes by hand, make sure they include the full name of the person they are interviewing, the place their interview was conducted, and the date. In all cases, have them ask permission to use their interview as part of a report that will be shared with others.

Questions you might suggest students include in their interviews:

1. What year were you born? How old were you in 1929 when the stock market crashed?

2. Where did you live during the Depression?

3. Did you live on a farm, in a small town, or in a city?

4. Who lived with you in your family when you were a child?

5. How did your family support itself? Who worked? What type of work did they do?

6. Did the Depression affect the day-to-day life of your family? If so, how? If not, why not?

7. Did you know what the Depression meant when you were a child?

8. Did the Depression have a direct effect on your life as a child?

9. Did the Depression influence how you thought about things or did things throughout your life?

10. Is there anything else you would like to tell me about the Depression?

Students can share their results in the form of a formal written report about the interview or by presenting an oral presentation describing the experience of the person they interviewed.

Students can extend this activity by exploring other significant events in the experience of their family.

ACTIVITY 28

Family Photographs

INTRODUCTION

Primary documents are remarkable sources that have the power to engage historians and students alike in a manner that textbooks or other secondary sources cannot hope to achieve. Unfortunately, most students are intimidated by primary documents and are never presented with opportunities to work with them.

Therefore, it is important not only to introduce students to working with primary documents but to do so using documents that they will be comfortable with. At the same time, students can be reminded of the roles that people in their own lives have played in the history being studied in their textbooks. Using family photographs can help serve both purposes at once.

ACTIVITY

Have students ask if their family has an album or a collection of old photographs. If they do, have them find out as much as they can about the photographs and the people in them. Where possible, students should discuss the photographs with people who were in them or took them. Where this is not possible, encourage students to consider the emotions and context of each photograph; allow them to develop their own story even if they are not certain that it is entirely historically accurate.

Request that students bring to class a few of their favorite photographs, photocopies being perfectly acceptable.

Either in groups or as an entire class, discuss with the students what their family photographs tell them about their family's history and experience.

Students can work with each other to create short family histories and attempt to fit these histories into the context of the classroom and its topics.

Discuss with the students how researching their own family histories using old photographs is related to working with actual primary documents in settings such as libraries or archives.

Extension: Students could take another family's photographic album and write a description of the family based on its images.

ACTIVITY 29

Women's Rights

INTRODUCTION

Elizabeth Cady Stanton, seated, and Susan B. Anthony, standing. Courtesy of the Library of Congress.

On July 14, 1848, the *Seneca County Courier*, a weekly paper published in Upstate New York, ran a brief advertisement inviting women to participate in a discussion of "the social, civil, and religious rights of women." The meeting, known as the Seneca Falls Convention and led by Elizabeth Cady Stanton (1815–1902) and Susan B. Anthony (1820–1906), is considered by most historians to be the beginning of the women's rights movement in the United States. The most important document produced at the convention was "The Declaration of Sentiments," which was closely modeled after the Declaration of Independence.

**The Declaration of Sentiments
From the Seneca Falls Convention, 1848**

When, in the course of human events, it becomes necessary for one portion of the family of man to assume among the people of the earth a position different from that which they have hitherto occupied, but one to which the laws of nature and of nature's God entitles them, a decent respect to the opinions of mankind requires that they should declare the causes that impel them to such a course.

We hold these truths to be self-evident: that all men and women are created equal; that they are endowed by their Creator with certain inalienable rights; that among these are life, liberty, and the pursuit of happiness; that to secure these rights governments are instituted, deriving their just powers from the consent of the governed. Whenever any form of government becomes destructive of these ends, it is the right of those who suffer from it to refuse allegiance to it, and to insist upon the institution of a new government, laying its foundation on such principles, and organizing its powers in such form, as to them shall seem most likely to effect their safety and happiness. Prudence indeed, will dictate that governments long established should not be changed for light and transient

---

causes; and accordingly all experience hath shown that mankind are more disposed to suffer, while evils are sufferable than to right themselves by abolishing the forms to which they were accustomed. But when a long train of abuses and usurpations, pursuing invariably the same object evinces a design to reduce them under absolute despotism, it is their duty to throw off such government, and to provide new guards for their future security. Such has been the patient sufferance of the women under this government, and such is now the necessity which constrains them to demand the equal station to which they are entitled.

The history of mankind is a history of repeated injuries and usurpations on the part of man toward woman, having in direct object the establishment of an absolute tyranny over her. To prove this, let facts be submitted to a candid world.

He has never permitted her to exercise her inalienable right to the elective franchise.

He has compelled her to submit to laws, in the formation of which she had no voice.

He has withheld from her rights which are given to the most ignorant and degraded men—both natives and foreigners.

Having deprived her of this first right of a citizen, the elective franchise, thereby leaving her without representation in the halls of legislation, he has oppressed her on all sides.

He has made her, if married, in the eyes of the law, civilly dead.

He has taken from her all right in property, even to the wages she earns.

He has made her, morally, an irresponsible being, as she can commit many crimes with impunity, provided they be done in the presence of her husband. In the covenant of marriage, she is compelled to promise obedience to her husband, he becoming, to all intents and purposes, her master—the law giving him power to deprive her of her liberty, and to administer chastisement.

He has so framed the laws of divorce, as to what shall be the proper causes, and in case of separation, to whom the guardianship of the children shall be given, as to be wholly regardless of the happiness of women—the law, in all cases, going upon a false supposition of the supremacy of man, and giving all power into his hands.

After depriving her of all rights as a married woman, if single, and the owner of property, he has taxed her to support a government which recognizes her only when her property can be made profitable to it.

He has monopolized nearly all the profitable employments, and from those she is permitted to follow, she receives but a scanty remuneration. He closes against her all the avenues to wealth and distinction which he considers most honorable to himself. As a teacher of theology, medicine, or law, she is not known.

He has denied her the facilities for obtaining a thorough education, all colleges being closed against her.

He allows her in Church, as well as State, but a subordinate position, claiming Apostolic authority for her exclusion from the ministry, and with some exceptions, from any public participation in the affairs of the Church.

He has created a false public sentiment by giving to the world a different code of morals for men and women, by which moral delinquencies which exclude women from society, are not only tolerated, but demand of little account in man.

(Continued)

(Continued)

He has usurped the prerogative of Jehovah himself, claiming it as his right to assign for her a sphere of action, when that belongs to her conscience and her God.

He has endeavored, in every way that he could, to destroy her confidence in her own powers, to lessen her self-respect, and to make her willing to lead a dependent and abject life. `

Now, in view of this entire disfranchisement of one-half the people of this country, their social and religious degradation—in view of the unjust laws above mentioned, and because women do feel themselves aggrieved, oppressed, and fraudulently deprived of their most sacred rights, we insist that they have immediate admission to all the rights and privileges which belong to them as citizens of the United States.

In entering upon the great work before us, we anticipate no small amount of misconception, misrepresentation, and ridicule; but we shall use every instrumentality within our power to effect our object. We shall employ agents, circulate tracts, petition the State and National legislatures, and endeavor to enlist the pulpit and the press in our behalf. We hope this Convention will be followed by a series of Conventions in every part of the country.

WHEREAS, The great precept of nature is conceded to be, that "man shall pursue his own true and substantial happiness." Blackstone in his Commentaries remarks, that his law of Nature being coeval with mankind, and dictated by God himself, is of course superior in obligation to any other. It is binding over all the globe, in all countries and at all times; no human laws are of any validity if contrary to this, and such of them as are valid, derive all their force, and all their validity, and all their authority, mediately and immediately, for this original; therefore,

RESOLVED, That such laws which prevent women from occupying such a station in society as her conscience shall dictate, or which places her in a position inferior to that of man, are contrary to the great precept of nature, and therefore of no force or authority.

RESOLVED, That woman is man's equal—was intended to be so by the Creator, and the highest good of the race demands that she such be recognized as such.

RESOLVED, That the women of this country ought to be enlightened in regard to the laws under which they live, that they may no longer publish their degradation by declaring themselves satisfied with their present position, nor their ignorance, by asserting that they have all the rights they want.

RESOLVED, That inasmuch as man, while claiming for himself intellectual superiority, does accord to woman moral superiority, it is pre-eminently his duty to encourage her to speak and teach, as she has an opportunity, in all religious assemblies.

RESOLVED, That the same amount of virtue, delicacy, and refinement of behavior that is required of woman in the social state, should also be required of man, and the same transgressions should be visited with equal severity on both man and woman.

RESOLVED, That the objection of indelicacy and impropriety, which is so often brought against woman when she addresses a public audience comes with a very ill-grace from those who encourage, by their attendance, her appearance on the stage, in the concert, or in feats of the circus.

RESOLVED, That woman has too long rested satisfied in the circumscribed limits which corrupt customs and a perverted application of the Scriptures have marked out for her, and that it is time she should move in the enlarged sphere which her great Creator has assigned her.

RESOLVED, That it is the duty of the women of this country to secure to themselves their sacred right to the elective franchise.

RESOLVED, That the equality of human rights results necessarily from the fact of the identity of the race in capabilities and responsibilities.

RESOLVED, That the speedy success of our cause depends upon the zealous and untiring efforts of both men and women, for the overthrow of the monopoly of the pulpit, and for the securing to woman an equal participation with men in the various trades, professions, and commerce.

RESOLVED, THEREFORE, That being invested by the Creator with the same capabilities, and the same consciousness of responsibility for their exercise, it is demonstrably the right and duty of woman, equally with man, to promote every righteous cause by every righteous means; and especially in regard to the great subjects of morals and religion, it is self-evidently her right to participate with her brother in teaching them, both in private and in public, by writing and by speaking, by instrumentalities proper to be used, and in any assemblies proper to be held; and in being a self-evident truth growing out of the divinely implanted principles of human nature, any custom or authority adverse to it, whether modern or wearing the hoary sanction of antiquity, is to be regarded as a self-evident falsehood, and at war with mankind.

ACTIVITY

Have students write a one-page editorial for the *Seneca County Courier* Labor Day issue of 1850. Have students focus on why, or why not, the principles of the Seneca Falls Convention should be supported.

Extension: Have students (both men and women) discuss how their lives would be different if the suffragists had not gained greater rights for women. For example, would a male student's mother have been able to have a job without the suffragists' efforts.

ACTIVITY 30

Today in History

INTRODUCTION

One of the more interesting Web sites available at the American Memory project through the Library of Congress is "Today in History." The library's staff has compiled extensive materials describing what happened for each calendar day of the year in our history. Included below is a sample from the American Memory "Today in History" collection for December 17, the anniversary of the first powered flight in history (Library of Congress).

First Flight, December 17, 1903

John T. Daniels, photographer.

Prints and Photographs Division

American Treasures of the Library of Congress

On the morning of **December 17**, 1903, **Wilbur and Orville Wright** took turns piloting and monitoring their flying machine in Kill Devil Hills, North Carolina. Orville piloted the first flight that lasted just twelve seconds. On the fourth and final flight of the day, Wilbur traveled 852 feet, remaining airborne for 57 seconds. That morning the brothers became the first people to demonstrate sustained flight of a heavier-than-air machine under the complete control of the pilot.

They had built the 1903 Flyer in sections in the back room of their Dayton, Ohio, bicycle shop. That afternoon, the Wright brothers walked the four miles to Kitty Hawk and sent a telegram to their father, Bishop Milton Wright, back home in Dayton:

Form No. 168.

THE WESTERN UNION TELEGRAPH COMPANY.

INCORPORATED

23,000 OFFICES IN AMERICA.   CABLE SERVICE TO ALL THE WORLD.

This Company TRANSMITS and DELIVERS messages only o... conditions limiting its liability, which have been assented to by the sender of the following message. Errors can be guarded against only by repeating a message back to the sending station for comparison, and the Company will not hold itself liable for errors or delays in transmission or delivery of Unrepeated Messages, beyond the amount of tolls paid thereon, nor in any case where the claim is not presented in writing within sixty days after the message is filed with the Company for transmission.
This is an UNREPEATED MESSAGE, and is delivered by request of the sender, under the conditions named above.
ROBERT C. CLOWRY, President and General Manager.

RECEIVED at   170

176 C KA CS 33 Paid.   Via Norfolk Va

Kitty Hawk N C Dec 17

Bishop M Wright

                    7 Hawthorne St

Success four flights thursday morning all against twenty one mile

wind started from Level with engine power alone average speed

through air thirty one miles longest 57 seconds inform Press

home ~~Xmas~~ Christmas .   Orevelle Wright   525P

American Memory can be found at http://memory.loc.gov/ammem/today/today.html.

Ensure that the class will have the opportunity to work with enough computers. If there are not enough computers available for each student to have his or her own, partner students into groups of two and instruct them to work together.

ACTIVITY

Have students visit the American Memory Project's "Today in History" Web site and use the archive to compile a one-page report of a major event that took place on their birthday. Have students include or make reference to original documents, including photographs.

Break students into groups of three (or three partners) and give an opportunity to share their discoveries. Emphasize that the students do not simply have to review their report but can discuss what they found most exciting in their research or how it feels to know that this event occurred on their birthday.

Extension: Have students create a "This Day in History" for their local community.

ACTIVITY 31

Photographs of the Farm Security Administration

Fishermen, Key West, Florida. Rothstein, Arthur, 1915, photographer. Created/Published Jan. 1938. Reproduction Number LC-USF33-T01-002700-M4 DLC (b&w film dup. neg.).

INTRODUCTION

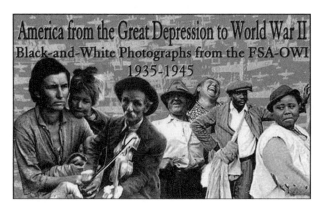

The Farm Security Administration (FSA) was a New Deal agency established in 1935 by the federal government. Its purpose was to develop and administer programs to aid destitute farmers and farm workers during the Great Depression. Photographers employed in the agency's Historical Section described economic and social conditions in America, especially in hard-hit rural areas, as well as the various activities of the agency. The FSA photographs are the most famous series of photographs to come out of the Great Depression of the 1930s. They are an extraordinary record of the American experience. In Florida, FSA photographers traveled throughout the farm areas, taking pictures of migrants and their families, of farmers laid low by hard times, and of decrepit houses and ruined land. In addition, the director of the photography project, Roy Emerson Stryker, encouraged FSA photographers in Florida to document life in wealthy and middle-class enclaves as well as in tourist camps along the coast. This additional coverage was unique and, combined with the images made of the crisis in the farming regions, provides contemporary viewers with a compelling and wide-ranging view of the state as it was a half century ago.

The FSA photographs are preserved in the Prints and Photography Division of the Library of Congress as part of the American Memory Project. Approximately 270,000 images are included as part of the collection. About 55,000 of the black-and-white images from the collection are now available online as well as 1,600 color photographs.

ACTIVITY

Have students visit the FSA Web site at the Library of Congress (http://memory.loc .gov/ammem/fsahtml/fahome.html), and have them search for photographs of their community. Have them discover if they can find the places where the FSA photographs were taken. Then have them take photographs of the same place. Have the students bring their images back to class along with images printed from the FSA Web site. Discuss how things have changed or remained the same in the seventy to seventy-five years since the photographs were first taken.

If photographs of the student's local community are not available, have them compare images from the FSA and the present for a large city such as New York. Contemporary images can be found on the Internet for comparison.

Extension: Have students create a photographic survey of their local community for future generations. This can be archived in the school library or with a local historical organization as well as posted as a Web site.

ACTIVITY 32

Primary and Secondary Sources

BILL OF PRICES,
AGREED ON BY THE
BRICK-LAYERS OF CINCINNATI,
MARCH 1, 1814.

	Dolls. Cts.
Brick laid (labor only) for brick & half walls, per thousand,	3 00
Do. for all exterior 9 inch walls, per thousand,	3 50
Do. for the 3d story of houses, per thousand, extra,	1 00
For finding lime, sand, loam and water, per thousand,	1 00
Outside arches, in front, common size, extra,	1 50
Back and side arches, outside, do. do.	1 00
For all inside arches, do.	50
Brick cornice, per foot, running, do.	25
Oiling and Penciling per yard, superficial,	12 1-2
For setting door sills,	1 00
For trimmers, common size,	1 00
For laying hearths, do.	1 00
Brick pa... ...ward, superficial,	18 3-4
For filling-in with brick, do.	18 3-4
Ovens, 3 feet by 2 feet 6 inches, or under, each,	5 00
Do. larger, per foot in depth,	2 00
Chimneys to frame houses, per thousand, counted solid,	4 00

Walls, laid Flemish bond, to be counted solid in all cases.
All other walls, doors and windows *only*, to be deducted.
The number of brick to be ascertained by counting them after they are laid.
Scaffold-boards and cords to be found by the employer.
    We, the subscribers, have duly considered the above prices as low as can be worked for.

ISAAC STAGG,   SAMUEL BROADWELL,
LOFTUS KEATING,   NATHAN DICKS,
JABEZ C. TUNIS,   ELIAS FISHER,
JONATHAN PANCOAST,   JOSEPH PANCOAST.
HENRY CRAVEN,

CINCINNATI—PRINTED BY LOOKER AND WALLACE.

INTRODUCTION

Historians typically deal with two types of sources for their research: primary and secondary. Primary sources are the records of an event or a period of time produced by those who witnessed or took part in the event. Primary sources include photographs, interviews, diaries, letters, speeches, literary works, autobiographies, and other materials. Secondary sources are one step removed from primary sources. Secondary sources tend to be more general and draw on primary sources as well as other secondary sources for their compilation. Secondary sources include text-books, histories, and encyclopedias.

ACTIVITY

Ask a few students to go to the back of the room and look toward the back wall or to go out into the hall for a moment. When these students are not looking, do an unusual activity (such as throwing the eraser at the wall). Ask the students who saw this to immediately write down what happened. When they are finished (within a minute or two), have them tell the other students what happened and have that group then attempt to write down what just happened. Explain that this differentiation is what separates primary and secondary sources.

Have students write an eyewitness or primary source account of an event. It could be of a class that you teach or of a school event such as a lunch period in the cafeteria. Have them observe and record events that took place. Limit observations and interviews to a specified amount of time—for example, one lunch period. In the case of lunch in the cafeteria, have students interview different people about what took place by having them talk to

1. Food staff

2. Students eating

3. Monitors

4. Teachers

Have students write a detailed two-page account of what they observed. In class, have students review what they observed—noting consistencies and inconsistencies between what they reported.

Variation: Have students report an event and then use one another's reports to write a history of what occurred. Distribute four or five reports of a particular event written by different students to each student. Have them come back with a one-page description of what occurred. Have students discuss with one another why they emphasized certain information in their reports. Discuss how their reports, based on the same sources, differ from one another.

ACTIVITY 33

Thinking Outside the Box

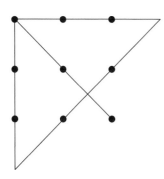

INTRODUCTION

A good follow-up to the Columbus egg problem is the puzzle that has you connect nine dots using only four lines while not lifting your pencil from the paper. Most people try to figure out the problem by staying within the boundaries of the dots. This does not work. What is needed is to "think outside the box." In other words, to extend the line beyond the boundaries of the dots. Then the solution to the puzzle becomes very simple.

ACTIVITY

Put the nine dots on the board and have students solve this problem for the fun of it.

When all students are finished (or are stuck) explain how to do the puzzle and then have them discuss how we get trapped into thinking about things in ways that can limit us. Encourage them to develop methods for solving problems that do not always have traditional solutions. Talk with them about why some people might be uncomfortable with such alternative approaches.

Extension: Have students perform this activity with their friends or family. Have students pay particular attention to how the individuals react to the puzzle and how something so simple (once you know the "trick") can seem so complex to someone who cannot see "outside of the box." Have students write up their reflections on this phenomenon of being able to see things from a completely different perspective.

ACTIVITY 34

Riddles

INTRODUCTION

Riddles have been told since ancient times. One of the most famous riddles is the riddle of the Sphinx. It plays an important part in the story of King Oedipus, which was the most famous play of the Greek playwright Sophocles. The riddle is asked by the Sphinx, a winged creature with the head of a woman and the body of a lion. The Sphinx ate whoever couldn't answer her riddle, which was, "What has one voice and yet becomes four-footed and two-footed and three-footed?" Answer: A person. A child crawls on all fours, an adult walks on two feet, and an old person uses a cane. This riddle reveals that a fundamental structure of riddles is that they are word puzzles that require lateral thinking (looking at an idea from a different perspective).

ACTIVITY

Tell students the Sphinx riddle and together talk through how and why it is considered a "riddle."

Have students create their own riddles. Share student creations with one another. Have students critique the riddles based on whether they are funny, insightful, clever, annoying, or complex. The following are some examples of riddles to help students get started with their own creations:

1. What always ends everything?

   Answer: The letter g

2. What is white, lives at the North Pole, and runs around naked?

   Answer: A Polar Bare

3. What does Santa give a 600 lb. gorilla for Christmas?

   Answer: Whatever it wants

4. Can you spell "hard water" only using three letters?

   Answer: Ice

Extension: Have students create a "top 10" riddle book for your class, one that can be shared with other classes, friends, or peers. Consider putting on a riddle performance or a "riddle game" to see who can out-riddle the other team (much like in Jeopardy).

ACTIVITY 35

Exploring Community Festivals

INTRODUCTION

Throughout the United States, there are thousands of local festivals and celebrations each year. Often, these celebrations are connected to local historical traditions, ethnic populations, and geographical legacies. They include everything from the Antique Gas and Steam Engine Show in Kentucky to the Pendleton Rodeo and Harvest Festival in Oregon and the Prince Lot Hula Festival in Hawaii. A list and description of these local community festivals can be found at the Community Roots Web site (www.loc.gov/folklife/roots/ac-home.html).

Included on this Web site are over 1,000 local legacies projects from all 50 states, the trusts, territories, and the District of Columbia. The site includes extensive photographs, written reports, sound and video recordings, newspaper clippings, posters, and other materials.

ACTIVITY

Have students visit the Web site at the Library of Congress and identify a local or regional celebration that interests them. Then have students attend local festivals on their own and in individual groups. They can create general reports on the overall festivals they attend or on individual activities they observe or possibly even participate in.

Extension: Have students attend a local festival and take photographs or record the event. Have them create an electronic report with the material they have collected.

ACTIVITY 36

Rebuses and Concrete Writing

TROUBLE

TROUBLE

(Double Trouble)

INTRODUCTION

There is a tradition of concrete writing, sometimes described as a *rebus*, in which a word literally looks like what it means. Look at the following examples:

SECRET

SECRET

SECRET

(Answer: Top Secret)

4INSTANCE

(Answer: For Instance)

CUT

CUT CUT CUT CUT CUT

(Answer: Cut Above the Rest)

HEAD

HEELS

(Answer: head over heels)

ACTIVITY

Provide students with a worksheet of such rebuses or put them up on the board. Give students five minutes to see how many of them they can solve.

Have students use rebuses to create concrete poems or stories—that is, that literally look like the words and things that they spell.

Extension: Have students create pictorial rebuses or hieroglyphics—for example, a picture of an eye to represent the pronoun *I*.

ACTIVITY 37

Mnemonics

INTRODUCTION

Mnemonics are memory aids. They help us to remember different types of information. Here are some examples of useful mnemonics used in science.

Order of colors in the rainbow, or visual spectrum:

Red, Orange, Yellow, Green, Blue, Indigo, Violet

Roy G. Biv

Order of taxonomy in biology:

Kingdom, Phylum, Class, Order, Family, Genus, Species

Kids Prefer Cheese Over Fried Green Spinach.

Order of geological time periods:

Cambrian, Ordovician, Silurian, Devonian, Carboniferous, Permian, Triassic, Jurassic, Cretaceous, Paleocene, Eocene, Oligocene, Miocene, Pliocene, Pleistocene, Recent

Cows Often Sit Down Carefully. Perhaps Their Joints Creak? Persistent Early Oiling Might Prevent Painful Rheumatism.

Order of Mohs hardness scale, from 1 to 10:

Talc, Gypsum, Calcite, Fluorite, Apatite, Orthoclase feldspar, Quartz, Topaz, Corundum, Diamond

Toronto Girls Can Flirt, And Other Queer Things Can Do.

The order of planets in average distance from the Sun:

Mercury, Venus, Earth, Mars, Jupiter, Saturn, Uranus, Neptune, Pluto (which some people now call a minor planet)

My Very Easy Method: Just Set Up Nine Planets.

ACTIVITY

Have students create useful mnemonic devices to help them memorize important information.

Extension: Have students explore how logos and rhyming jingles in advertisements are examples of mnemonic devices. Have them collect examples found in the culture.

ACTIVITY 38

Designing a Memorial

INTRODUCTION

Memorials are an important part of our life and culture. We use them to commemorate important historical events or people famous or less well known. Think about a cemetery. Its tombstones and mausoleums are memorials to the people who are buried in them.

Some of the most famous memorials in the United States are in Washington, D.C. and include the Washington Memorial, the Lincoln Memorial, the Jefferson Memorial, and the Vietnam War Memorial.

Lincoln Memorial

ACTIVITY

Have students design a memorial for a famous person (Martin Luther King) or for a cause (women's suffrage). Students can present and display their memorials. Other students can critique their effectiveness as designs.

Extension: Have students find a memorial in their own town and create a map and bulletin board display or a Web site describing it (look in town squares, parks, etc.). Have them conduct a similar project about a local cemetery that is of historical interest.

ACTIVITY 39

Stepping Into a Painting

INTRODUCTION

In the Harry Potter books and films, paintings at the Hogwarts School literally come alive. Using their imaginations, students can do the same thing by taking a famous painting and using it as the basis for constructing a story or historical account based on the information contained in the image.

Ensure that the class will have the opportunity to work with enough computers. If there are not enough computers available for each student to have his or her own, partner students into groups of two and instruct them to work together.

ACTIVITY

Have students visit the Web site of the National Gallery of Art in Washington, D.C. (www.nga.gov), and select a painting around which they wish to create an imaginative story or a historical account. You can start them off with a painting such as Edward Hicks, *Peaceable Kingdom* (ca. 1834), one of the most famous American paintings included in the National Gallery of Art.

Break students into groups of three (or three partners) and give the groups an opportunity to share their stories with each other. Emphasize that the format or absurdity of their stories is not as important as their use of information contained within the image.

Extension: Reverse the process and have students create a picture based on a famous story or book that they know, such as *Robinson Crusoe* or *Charlotte's Web.*

ACTIVITY 40

Japanese Internment During World War II

INTRODUCTION

During World War II, 112,000 to 120,000 Japanese and Japanese Americans were sent to prison or war relocation camps in the United States. A total of 62 percent of those who were sent to these camps were U.S. citizens from the West Coast. Eventually, the U.S. government (in the 1980s) apologized for the internment, saying that it was based on "race prejudice, war hysteria, and a failure of political leadership." Reparations were paid to survivors.

Many feel that the payment of reparations for past social injustices is not an effective means of compensation for individuals whose families historically have been unfairly treated. Should reparations, for example, be available for people of African American descent as a result of their ancestors having suffered under slavery?

Oakland, California, Feb. 1942. Attributed to Dorothea Lange. Courtesy of the Library of Congress.

ACTIVITY

Organize students to debate the issue pro and con, each presenting arguments for and against the use of reparations.

Have them write brief position papers arguing for and against each side of the debate.

Extension: Discuss with students who have been demonstrably discriminated against in American culture if they should be provided with reparations for past injustices.

ACTIVITY 41

ASCII Code

INTRODUCTION

Computers are based on the use of binary code, in which information is processed using 0s or 1s. In the computational part of the computer, this translates into positive or negative electrical impulses (pluses or minuses).

Using 0s or 1s (pluses or minuses), the computer can express any numerical value as its binary translation. To represent letters and other non-numeric characters, computers use *ASCII tables*, which are tables or lists that contain all the letters in the roman alphabet plus some additional characters. In the ASCII tables, each character is represented by the same order number. The ASCII code for the capital letter "A," for example, is always represented by the order number 65, which is expressed in binary code as 1000001.

ACTIVITY

The chart on the following page contains the capital letters A through Z in ASCII code. Reproduce the chart and have students use it to write coded messages to one another. Have them start by translating the following statement, which is written in binary (the eight digit code of 0s and 1s assigned to each letter and symbol included in ASCII code). The binary code is in the final column before the letter it represents. Remember each line found below is a word.

01010100 01001000 01001001 01010011

01001001 01010011

01000001

01000011 01001111 01000100 01000101 01000100

01001101 01000101 01010011 01010011 01000001 01000111 01000101

Capital Letters A–Z in ASCII Code

065 101 041 01000001 A

066 102 042 01000010 B

067 103 043 01000011 C

068 104 044 01000100 D

069 105 045 01000101 E

070 106 046 01000110 F

071 107 047 01000111 G

072 110 048 01001000 H

073 111 049 01001001 I

074 112 04A 01001010 J

075 113 04B 01001011 K

076 114 04C 01001100 L

077 115 04D 01001101 M

078 116 04E 01001110 N

079 117 04F 01001111 O

080 120 050 01010000 P

081 121 051 01010001 Q

082 122 052 01010010 R

083 123 053 01010011 S

084 124 054 01010100 T

085 125 055 01010101 U

086 126 056 01010110 V

087 127 057 01010111 W

088 130 058 01011000 X

089 131 059 01011001 Y

090 132 05A 01011010 Z

Discuss with students how they could go about decoding the preceding message if they didn't have the chart of ASCII letters to work with.

Extension: Have students analyze the number of letters, objects, or things that could be represented by one 0 and one 1, by two of each number, and so on.

ACTIVITY 42

Protest Songs

We Shall Overcome

1.
We shall overcome
We shall overcome
We shall overcome some day

CHORUS:
Oh, deep in my heart
I do believe
We shall overcome some day

2.
We'll walk hand in hand
We'll walk hand in hand
We'll walk hand in hand some day
CHORUS

3.
We shall all be free
We shall all be free
We shall all be free some day
CHORUS

4.
We are not afraid
We are not afraid
We are not afraid some day
CHORUS

5.
We are not alone
We are not alone
We are not alone some day
CHORUS

6.
The whole wide world around
The whole wide world around
The whole wide world around some day
CHORUS

7.
We shall overcome
We shall overcome
We shall overcome some day
CHORUS

INTRODUCTION

"We Shall Overcome" is based on Charles Tindley's gospel song "I'll Overcome Some Day" (1900), with its opening and closing melody from the nineteenth-century spiritual "No More Auction Block for Me" (a Black spiritual that dates to before the Civil War). It became the unofficial anthem of the Civil Rights Movement in the United States. Its lyrics are included in the box above.

Protest songs are written to protest and bring attention to problems in society ranging from injustice to racial discrimination and war. They have a long history in the United States, going back to at least the time of the American Revolution.

ACTIVITY

Have students use the Internet to research the lyrics for different protest songs using the search phrase "protest songs." After looking at examples of protest songs, have students write their own songs for an issue that interests them. They should create their own lyrics, and if they are musicians, create their own music. If they are not musicians, have them put words to an existing tune.

Extension: Have students experiment with other means of expressing their opposition. For example, have them write a political broadside.

ACTIVITY 43

Inaugural Presidential Address

INTRODUCTION

Presidential inaugural addresses represent some of the most important moments in American history. Students can explore the content of presidential addresses by visiting the Library of Congress Web site "I Do Solemnly Swear . . .": Presidential Inaugurations (http://memory .loc.gov/ammem/pihtml/pihome.html), which includes thousands of items relating to inaugurations (diaries and letters of presidents and of those who witnessed inaugurations, handwritten drafts of inaugural addresses, broadsides, inaugural tickets and programs, prints, photographs, and sheet music) from George Washington in 1789 to George W. Bush's inauguration of 2001.

ACTIVITY

Have students research specific presidential inaugurations, discovering what the key issues were for the period in which they occurred. Students can create written and oral reports, Web sites, and bulletin board displays for the inaugurations they are studying.

Extension: Have students create a list of five important topics or issues they feel should be included in the next presidential inauguration speech.

ACTIVITY 44

Portals to the World

INTRODUCTION

The Library of Congress has established a Portals to the World Web site (www.loc.gov/rr/inter national/portals.html) that contains basic introductions and links to in-depth information about the nations and other areas of the world.

ACTIVITY

Have students visit this site to develop an oral or written report on a specific country. Have them assume the role of "ambassador" or an expert from a country, capable of providing a detailed overview of a country and why it is of interest.

Extension: Have students create a similar report about a neighborhood or place in their local community.

ACTIVITY 45

Stories From Childhood

INTRODUCTION

Memories of childhood can be a rich source of information. In fact, many authors have used their childhood experience as the basis for developing some of their most important writing. This is the case with Samuel Clemens (aka Mark Twain), for example, whose most important work, *Huckleberry Finn*, was based to a significant extent on memories of his childhood in Hannibal, Missouri.

ACTIVITY

Take a place from your childhood (a house where you lived, a classroom in which you were a student, a favorite vacation spot for your family, or your grandparent's house) or an event (a trip to another city, the illness of a friend) and use it to write an original story. For example, maybe you went to a videogame arcade and played a game like *Galaxians* in which space invaders attack your planet. You could create a story in which real aliens transport themselves into the video game and you have to fight against them to save the planet. Maybe you had a special cat or dog. You could make your pet into a character who talks about the people he or she sees from the animal's perspective. The English author Saki (H. H. Munro, 1870–1914) did this in a famous story titled "Tobermory," in which a cat living in a country house learns to talk and starts repeating vicious comments guests at the house make about one another. The story ends with the guests killing the cat to keep him from repeating the nasty things they had said.

Extension: Have students create a story using their school and classroom as its location.

ACTIVITY 46

Round-Robin Stories

INTRODUCTION

Story telling is often an "additive" process in which people contribute elements as they build a narrative. This activity has students create a story by contributing its separate parts in a "round-robin" process to create a narrative.

ACTIVITY

Have students take out a paper and pencil and create the outline of a story in the following way. Begin "Once upon a time. . . ." Then ask a student for a subject: for example, "a man." Then ask for a verb: for example, "sailed." In doing so, you will be creating a story line. Keep up the process until students have a detailed outline from which to create a story. Your outline might look something like this:

> Once upon a time
> a man
> sailed
> from
> to
> and found . . .

Once the outline has been created, have students use it to create their own story. Using the outline above, for example, a story could go like this: "Once upon a time a man with cold blue eyes and hair gold as straw sailed from Jamaica to the secret pirate island. On the island he and his companions found. . . ."

Have students share their stories with each other. Discuss the differences and similarities in their stories. Create a collection of them online or on a bulletin board so that people can share and compare them.

Extension: Have students open a history book or encyclopedia, randomly turn to a page, and with their eyes closed point to a spot on the page. Whatever sentence is closest should then be used to begin a story.

ACTIVITY 47

Writing Grab Bag

INTRODUCTION

Students often have difficulty initiating a story. Using a
"writing grab bag" can help solve this problem by giving them a means by which to initiate the
imaginative process and actually write.

ACTIVITY

Write the names of different people, places, and things on 3 × 5 cards. Or you can paste a picture (downtown New York City, a waterfall, an airplane, etc.) to a card. Create fifteen or twenty cards.

Have students pull the cards from the bag and use them to outline and create a narrative thread for a story. Create the story as a group or class activity.

Extension: Students can craft their own individual stories using this process. Stories can be shared and compared or posted on bulletin boards or on Web sites.

ACTIVITY 48

Using Census Data

INTRODUCTION

The U.S. Constitution requires that a national census be taken every ten years. Censuses have been conducted since 1790. The data included in the various censuses have been invaluable to historians, allowing them a means by which to identify important shifts in work patterns and population growth. Census data also make it possible to see migration patterns, as well as the growth or decline of certain industries.

The U.S. Historical Census Data Browser (http://fisher .lib.virginia.edu/census) allows users to select specific census categories and find data at the county level.

ACTIVITY

Have students use the Data Browser to construct a profile of what their local community was like 150 years ago, 50 years ago, and so on. Have them construct profiles of specific population groups, such as African Americans, Chinese Americans, or women.

Students can develop classroom presentations based on the census data. More formal reports can be used to create a bulletin board or Web site about their county.

ACTIVITY 49

Explore a Favorite Artist

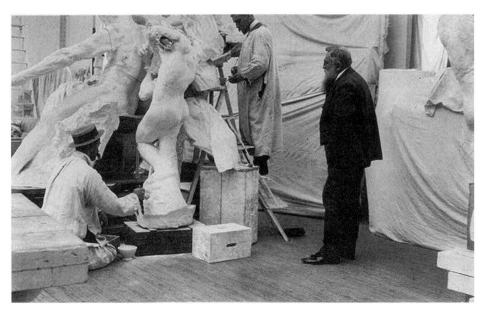

Auguste Rodin standing with sculptures and two assistants. Photograph by Frances Benjamin Johnston, 1905. Courtesy of the Library of Congress.

INTRODUCTION

Almost all of us have a favorite artist. Why we like one artist more than another is a very personal sort of thing and reflects our individual personalities and interests.

ACTIVITY

Have students decide on an artist they really like. Have them go online or use published sources to research the history of the artist.

After choosing three works they feel most represent the work of the artist they have chosen, students should write a brief report, which includes a biography and explanation of why these works are representative of the artist whom they have chosen.

Extension: Have students present their reports in class, assuming the personas of the artist they are reporting on ("My name is Vincent van Gogh, and . . .").

ACTIVITY 50

What Makes a Good Life?

INTRODUCTION

"What constitutes a good life?" is a question that has been asked in Western culture going back to the ancients. For a hungry child in the Great Depression, a good life was a bottle of milk and enough to eat.

Drought victim from Kentucky, in school with bottle of milk he received in a Red Cross lunch program, ca. 1930. Photograph by Lewis W. Hine. Courtesy of the Library of Congress.

ACTIVITY

Have students discuss what makes them happy and what makes them unhappy. Ask them to reflect on the essentials of happiness, identifying material and nonmaterial things necessary for the creation of a "good life." Have them each create a collage of words and images and then write a short explanation of why they consider these things necessary for a good life.

Extension: Have students share their thoughts with one another as part of small discussion groups.

ACTIVITY 51

Creating an Ethical Will

INTRODUCTION

An ethical will (*zevaoth*) is a Jewish custom of passing down certain precepts, ideas, or ethical principles from a father to a child or a teacher to a pupil. It was an attempt by the writer to pass down his or her most valued ideas and beliefs.

ACTIVITY

Ask students what is the most important thing they believe in that they would want to tell their friends. Explain the custom of an ethical will and how it was an important process of transmitting values across generations.

Have students consider the ways parents try to pass down their values from generation to generation. Have them develop a list of questions and ideas that they can use in a discussion with a parent or grandparent about creating an ethical will. For example, students might attempt to focus on the most important life lessons they would want to pass on to future generations or events in their parents' lives that are worth remembering.

For background on ethical wills visit the Ethical Wills Web site (www.ethicalwill.com) or read the Ethical Will article included in Wikipedia, which has many useful Web links (http://en.wikipedia.org/wiki/Ethical_will).

Extension: Have students go ahead and write an ethical will.

ACTIVITY 52

Written in Stone

INTRODUCTION

Cemeteries and tombstones are remarkable means for understanding the history of local communities. While tombstones are meant as points of remembrance, scholars have also long noted that tombstones and the process of burial are about the process of grieving by the living rather than a simple remembrance of those who have died. As such, what is written or shown on a tombstone says as much about those doing the burial as about the person being buried.

ACTIVITY

Have students visit local cemeteries to learn about local architecture and history. Have them imagine that they are from thousands of years in the future and that the cemetery is the only source of information that survives about our culture. What could they learn? Have them write a two- to three-page description of what information the cemetery and its resources provided them.

Extension: Have students go to a segment of the cemetery that is at least one hundred years old, randomly select twenty-five graves, and write down the average age of death for the people buried in them.

ACTIVITY 53

Photographic Timeline

(A)

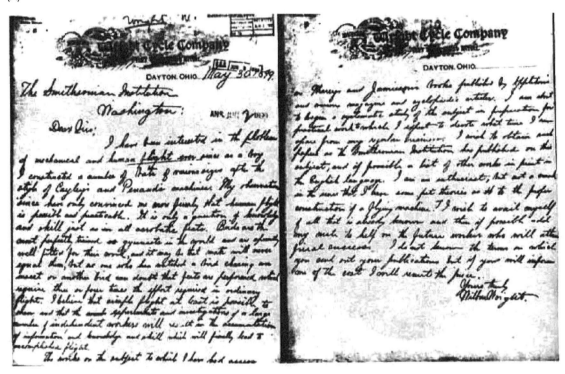

(A)   1899: The Wright Brothers write to the Smithsonian Institution for information about flying. Courtesy of the Library of Congress

(B)

(C)

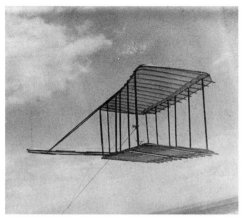

(B)   1900: They design their first glider and begin experimenting at Kitty Hawk, North Carolina. Courtesy of the Library of Congress
(C)   1903: The Wright Brothers make the first controlled powered flight on December 17. Courtesy of the Library of Congress

INTRODUCTION

Establishing a solid understanding of the past and what has preceded us is an important part of comprehending who and what we are as individuals.

ACTIVITY

Have students identify a historical period that is important to them (the Civil War, the 1960s, the Civil Rights Movement, etc.). Next, have them create a historical photographic timeline for a specific period or community.

Once students have completed this activity, have them discuss with one another whether the events included on their timelines still have significance to their contemporary experience. Have them consider what the consequences would be if the events they have outlined had not taken place.

Extension: Have students create a timeline for a very limited period of time, such as the time it took them to get to school this morning. Have them try to break down their timeline into the smallest units possible—perhaps as small as a minute or five minutes.

ACTIVITY 54

1900

INTRODUCTION

In 1900, there were no phones, planes, video games, televisions, or computers. Most people lived and died in the locale where they were born. Young children routinely went to work (for 10–12 hours a day) rather than to school, oftentimes in horrific conditions without proper food, clothing, or health and safety considerations.

ACTIVITY

Have students construct what the world was like in 1900. Use historical data as well as developing fictional first-person narratives to make this world more realistic and understandable. Have them write brief reports or do class presentations based on what they have found.

Extension: Have students imagine what their lives would be like without electricity or a phone or central heating. How would their lives be different?

ACTIVITY 55

Ninety-Five Theses

INTRODUCTION

In 1517, Martin Luther is said to have nailed a statement of ninety-five theses on the door of the Castle Church in Wittenberg, Germany. These theses ("The Disputation of Martin Luther on the Power and Efficacy of Indulgences") were a challenge to the Roman Catholic Church on issues such as the authority of the Pope and the nature of penance. Luther saw himself as advancing the true doctrine of the church even though his actions gave rise to the Protestant tradition, in many ways different from Catholicism.

ACTIVITY

Have students choose a current event (local, national, or global). Discuss the multiple issues and perspectives that surround this event.

Extension: Have students communicate their opinions about a current issue by developing and delivering a set of "theses" based on the concept of the "Ninety-Five Theses" written by Martin Luther. Limit yourself to five well-thought-out theses.

ACTIVITY 56

Analyzing The New England Primer (1692)

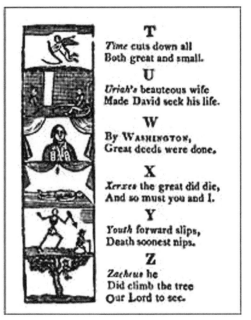

A sample page from the rhyming alphabet from an early edition of *The New England Primer*.

INTRODUCTION

The New England Primer is the most famous textbook to come from the Colonial era. Many full-length examples of it can be found online by typing "New England Primer" into a search engine like Google.

ACTIVITY

Go carefully through the primer and compile a list of items that you find interesting or worth noting. Have students use these items to compile a two- to three-page double-spaced essay describing what late Puritan culture must have been like in the Massachusetts Bay Colony. What did children learn? What instructional methods were evidently used? What things did the culture feel it was important to teach its children?

Extension: Have students examine a history or social studies textbook they are using. Ask them what their text might tell future historians about who and what we are as a people.

ACTIVITY 57

Slavery in the Constitution?

INTRODUCTION

No single document in recent history has received the intense scrutiny that the Constitution has been subjected to. Political groups, students, foreign governments, and the courts have all not just studied the Constitution but have endeavored to interpret and apply it to their lives and the world around them.

The Constitution has been subject to this piercing analysis since its publication, and one of the social issues about which America has turned to the Constitution is the institution of slavery. Remarkably, the actual word *slavery* does not appear anywhere in the document. At the same time, the institution is included in the Constitution and dealt with in several clauses.

ACTIVITY

Prepare copies of the Constitution of the United States Worksheet for students to work either individually or in groups of three to five. Group size should be kept as small as possible, with five being the absolute maximum. Any greater, and each student will not be able to participate at acceptable levels in the activity. An overhead projection version of the worksheet would also be helpful.

Assign students to groups (unless they will be working individually) and provide each group (or individual) with a worksheet. With as little explanation as possible, ask the students to search through the Constitution for the word *slavery*. Give them a moment or two to realize that the word itself is not found anywhere in the Constitution.

Next, have the students search the document for any reference to the institution of slavery. Allow them a few moments for this stage as these references can be difficult to spot and may require group thought processes in working out what qualifies and what does not. Afterward, go around the room and have the students report their findings until all references to slavery have been cited.

Discuss with students that many of the Founding Fathers responsible for the Constitution owned slaves. Make sure they are aware that while these men owned other individuals, they did recognize that perhaps this institution went against the values and rights that they were delineating in the Constitution.

Ask the students if they believe it would have been possible for the men at the Constitutional Convention to have outlawed slavery. Even though they chose not to, why were the delegates so careful in avoiding placing the actual term *slavery* into the Constitution?

Extension: Discuss with students that the Equal Rights Amendment (ERA) was originally drafted by Alice Paul in 1923. The amendment states, "Equality of rights under the law shall not be denied or abridged by the United States or by any State on account of sex." In 1982, the amendment failed to be ratified by a minimum of 38 states. It still remains to be ratified. Discuss whether or not there is still a need for such a constitutional amendment.

The Constitution of the United States of America

(abridged version)

We the people of the United States, in order to form a more perfect union, establish justice, insure domestic tranquility, provide for the common defense, promote the general welfare, and secure the blessings of liberty to ourselves and our posterity, do ordain and establish this Constitution for the United States of America.

Article I

Section 1. All legislative powers herein granted shall be vested in a Congress of the United States, which shall consist of a Senate and House of Representatives.

Section 2. The House of Representatives shall be composed of members chosen every second year by the people of the several states, and the electors in each state shall have the qualifications requisite for electors of the most numerous branch of the state legislature.

Representatives and direct taxes shall be apportioned among the several states which may be included within this union, according to their respective numbers, which shall be determined by adding to the whole number of free persons, including those bound to service for a term of years, and excluding Indians not taxed, three fifths of all other Persons. The actual Enumeration shall be made within three years after the first meeting of the Congress of the United States, and within every subsequent term of ten years, in such manner as they shall by law direct. The number of Representatives shall not exceed one for every thirty thousand, but each state shall have at least one Representative; and until such enumeration shall be made, the state of New Hampshire shall be entitled to choose three, Massachusetts eight, Rhode Island and Providence Plantations one, Connecticut five, New York six, New Jersey four, Pennsylvania eight, Delaware one, Maryland six, Virginia ten, North Carolina five, South Carolina five, and Georgia three.

Section 8. The Congress shall have power to lay and collect taxes, duties, imposts and excises, to pay the debts and provide for the common defense and general welfare of the United States; but all duties, imposts and excises shall be uniform throughout the United States;

To borrow money on the credit of the United States;

To regulate commerce with foreign nations, and among the several states, and with the Indian tribes;

To establish a uniform rule of naturalization, and uniform laws on the subject of bankruptcies throughout the United States;

To coin money, regulate the value thereof, and of foreign coin, and fix the standard of weights and measures;

To provide for the punishment of counterfeiting the securities and current coin of the United States;

To establish post offices and post roads;

To promote the progress of science and useful arts, by securing for limited times to authors and inventors the exclusive right to their respective writings and discoveries;

To define and punish piracies and felonies committed on the high seas, and offenses against the law of nations;

To declare war, grant letters of marquee and reprisal, and make rules concerning captures on land and water;

To raise and support armies, but no appropriation of money to that use shall be for a longer term than two years; To provide and maintain a navy;

To make rules for the government and regulation of the land and naval forces;

To provide for calling forth the militia to execute the laws of the union, suppress insurrections and repel invasions;

To provide for organizing, arming, and disciplining the militia and for governing such part of them as may be employed in the service of the United States, reserving to the states respectively, the appointment of the officers and the authority of training the militia according to the discipline prescribed by Congress;

Section 9. The migration or importation of such persons as any of the states now existing shall think proper to admit, shall not be prohibited by the Congress prior to the year one thousand eight hundred and eight, but a tax or duty may be imposed on such importation, not exceeding ten dollars for each person.

The privileges of the writ of habeas corpus shall not be suspended, unless when in cases of rebellion or invasion the public safety may require it.

No capitation, or other direct, tax shall be laid, unless in proportion to the census or enumeration herein before directed to be taken.

No tax or duty shall be laid on articles exported from any state.

No preference shall be given by any regulation of commerce or revenue to the ports of one state over those of another: nor shall vessels bound to, or from, one state, be obliged to enter, clear or pay duties in another.

No title of nobility shall be granted by the United States: and no person holding any office of profit or trust under them, shall, without the consent of the Congress, accept any present, emolument, office, or title, of any kind whatever, from any king, prince, or foreign state.

Article IV

Section 1. Full faith and credit shall be given in each state to the public acts, records, and judicial proceedings of every other state. And the Congress may by general laws prescribe the manner in which such acts, records, and proceedings shall be proved, and the effect thereof.

Section 2. The citizens of each state shall be entitled to all privileges and immunities of citizens in the several states.

A person charged in any state with treason, felony, or other crime, who shall flee from justice, and be found in another state, shall on demand of the executive authority of the state from which he fled, be delivered up, to be removed to the state having jurisdiction of the crime.

No person held to service or labor in one state, under the laws thereof, escaping into another, shall, in consequence of any law or regulation therein, be discharged from such service or labor, but shall be delivered up on the claim of the party to whom such service or labor may be due.

ACTIVITY 58

How Crowded Was the Middle Passage?

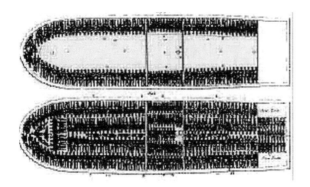

INTRODUCTION

Slavery is a legacy of American history that is at the same time hugely important to the present and remarkably challenging for everyday students to grasp in its entirety. Indeed, it may not be possible for the vast majority of Americans to truly understand just how brutal and dehumanizing the institution of slavery was for Africans and their descendants in the New World. No aspect of this experience is more distant from our own repertoire of experiences than the Middle Passage.

It would be difficult, and probably illegal, to attempt to fully re-create the Middle Passage within a public school classroom. Oral histories and slave narratives are of assistance, as are visuals such as the movie *Amistad*. Still, in at least one small way, teachers can demonstrate to students a little bit of the horrors of the slave ships. And any little bit helps.

ACTIVITY

Using common masking or duct tape, mark off columns on the floor of the classroom. Each strip of tape should be approximately twenty inches apart. If the class is older or has shown itself to be especially mature, each strip can be as close as fifteen inches apart. You will need enough room for your entire class to fit according to the following instructions, so make sure that you are preparing sufficient columns.

Once the class is in their seats and it is time for this activity to begin, instruct the students to move their desks or take whatever other actions necessary to provide enough room. Once space is cleared, have students lay down within the taped hash marks.

Depending on how maturely the class is handling the situation, you can begin discussing this experience while they are still on the floor, or you can have them return to their desks and then perform the postprocess. This will need to be a judgment call by you as the teacher who best understands each individual group of students.

Begin with the general questions of how students felt in such close proximity to their peers. Was there enough room to make themselves comfortable? Did they find it awkward to be so close to their neighbors? Was the floor a soft surface that was conducive to things like sleeping or relaxing?

Next explain that the experience they had lasted only for a few minutes. Have them reflect what it would have been like to be kept in much worse conditions for weeks and months. Point out that for the most part, slaves were stark naked on board the ship. Remind them also that the floors were often damp, or outright wet, and that the boat rocked—often tumultuously. If your hash marks were twenty inches apart, point out that most slaves were given only fifteen inches of space and therefore they had substantially less of a personal bubble than the students were just given.

Finally, explain to the students how long the slaves had to remain in this tiny space. Note the overall duration of the Middle Passage as well as the rarity with which slaves were permitted out of their holds. They had to eat, sleep, and often, go the restroom in the same fifteen inches of space.

Extension: Have students explore online contemporary human rights abuses and discuss whether or not they can do anything to help prevent such abuses.

ACTIVITY 59

The List of Creepy Coincidences

INTRODUCTION

One of the greatest rewards and, simultaneously, greatest challenges of history is connecting distant people, places, and events together through broad themes and patterns that can help us explain, sympathize with, and predict. Yet for many students, history is just that—the distant past. Its only function is to consume about fifty minutes a day of their lives for over ten years and fill their backpacks with weighty textbooks.

Sometimes it takes an extreme example for students to really get excited about connections in history. One such educational opportunity that will certainly grab the attention of students and likely get them energized about a little research is "The List of Creepy Coincidences."

The first of the two lists provided in this activity is a set of remarkable coincidences between Abraham Lincoln and John F. Kennedy. Both figures are popular historical heroes who most students are at least superficially familiar with. Some of the similarities between the two men stretch the truth; others are blatant mistruths. This, however, is for the moment not our concern.

With a starting point of such a bizarre bit of information, teachers can encourage students to become enthusiastic about researching and provide many their first motivation to truly delve into the school library, some online sources, or even a single source provided by the teacher.

Either prepare the two lists on the classroom board, being careful to cover the Fillmore/Truman list, or prepare a pair of overhead projection sheets with the lists on them.

The type of research you intend your students to perform after your presentation of the two lists will affect the additional preprocess preparations. For example, if you intend for the students to use the library of your school, you will need to ensure that this is possible. Or you could grab a few books from the library yourself on topics that you believe your students will enjoy researching.

ACTIVITY

To start the activity, eloquently complain to the students about how every year someone approaches you with a crazy conspiracy theory that he or she wishes you to explain. You should express surprise that this person would turn to a history teacher to explain a conspiracy. Then present the Lincoln/Kennedy list.

Allow a moment for the weirdness of the list to sink in. Ask the students what they think about the facts given and how much credibility they give to these strange coincidences. What could all this mean?

Next, show how such a list can be compiled about two much less prominent individuals. At this point, you can use the Fillmore/Truman list.

Finally, explain that such a list can be compiled no matter what two people are taken under consideration. They can be picked at random, and they do not have to be presidents. They could be actors, civil rights leaders, or shoe salesmen. Have students select a pair of historical figures whom they can research in an effort to compile a short list of creepy coincidences. This can be done in a variety of ways: group work or individual, at the library or in the classroom, during a class session or for homework. This will depend on your schedule, your school's resources, and your class itself.

The List of Creepy Coincidences

Between Abraham Lincoln and John F. Kennedy

1. Lincoln was elected to Congress in 1846. Kennedy was elected to Congress in 1946.
2. Lincoln was elected president in 1860. Kennedy was elected president in 1960.
3. The names Lincoln and Kennedy each contain seven letters.
4. Both presidents were shot in the head, on a Friday, before a major holiday.
5. Both presidents were assassinated by and succeeded by southerners.
6. Both successors were named Johnson, born in years ending in '08.
7. Both assassins were known by three names, born in years ending in '39.
8. Both assassins were murdered before their trial.
9. Booth ran from a theater and was caught in a warehouse; Oswald ran from a warehouse and was caught in a theater.
10. Lincoln had a secretary named Kennedy; Kennedy had a secretary named Lincoln.

The List of Creepy Coincidences

Between Millard Fillmore and Harry S. Truman

1. Fillmore's pioneer father owned a failing farm, and he helped run it as a young man. Truman's pioneer father owned a failing farm, and he helped run it as a young man.
2. Fillmore had an unsuccessful stint in the clothing industry, a failed fuller's apprentice. Truman had an unsuccessful stint in the clothing industry, a bankrupt haberdasher.
3. Fillmore joined the Whig Party in 1834; Truman joined the Democratic Party in 1934.
4. Both Fillmore and Truman won every election prior to the presidency, except one.
5. Fillmore was a New Yorker placed on the ticket to balance a candidate from the South. Truman was a southerner placed on the ticket to balance a candidate from New York.
6. Fillmore succeeded a war-hero general and was succeeded by a man named Franklin. Truman replaced a man named Franklin and was succeeded by a war-hero general.
7. Both presidents rose to their office soon after a major holiday.
8. Both became presidents during a national crisis, which concluded a few months later.
9. Both presidents left office highly unpopular without their party's nomination— Fillmore in 1853, Truman in 1953.
10. Fillmore was born on a Tuesday and died on the 8th. Truman was born on the 8th and died on a Tuesday.

Extension: Have students go online and search under the term "strange or amazing coincidences." Have them create a class collection of interesting coincidences.

ACTIVITY 60

Sacrifices

INTRODUCTION

Students today will lodge protests over prohibitions against exposed bellies or complain on a daily basis for a month if their locker time is reduced by so much as a minute. At home, compromise is often a thing of the past. Genuine sacrifice is almost unheard of.

From such a perspective, it is hard to relate to or even understand soldiers not much older than themselves who were willing to enter the trenches of World War I knowing that doing so came with a very high risk of receiving a wound. Death was something to be expected.

While we cannot re-create the trenches, we can push students to think about what in their lives is important and what sacrifices they would be willing to make to save those things.

For this activity, no advanced preparatory work should be required. Students will need only standard materials that they should have with them, including paper and pencil. If desired, the teacher can preselect the groups the students will break into.

ACTIVITY

Split students into groups of about four, and have each group designate a spokesperson and a recorder. The recorder will be responsible for keeping a list of two things: first, a few things the group feels are important to their lives; and second, the most the group would be willing to sacrifice for each of those things.

Make certain that students understand that the entire group must agree before something is put down onto the recorder's sheet. Group discussion and debate is highly encouraged.

Some examples, should you wish to provide them, would include the following: important things—school, friends, family, the president, America, freedom; sacrifices—life, mobile phone, kidney, an afternoon, an allowance, television.

After a few minutes, have each group spokesperson present two or three different things that their group was able to agree on.

Discuss with students how easy or difficult it was for groups to agree about not just what was important in their lives but about what they would be willing to trade for these things.

When you are ready to move on to relating this activity to the soldiers of World War I, ask the students what they think the soldiers who fought in that war would have listed. Do the students think that these soldiers (teenagers really) would have been willing to sacrifice their lives for these things before the war broke out?

Extension: Discuss with students the types of sacrifices people make as members of families. Explore why they are willing to make these sacrifices.

ACTIVITY 61

The Classroom Missile Crisis

INTRODUCTION

The Cold War is becoming increasingly a thing of the past. Students who were not even alive when the Berlin Wall came down are beginning to enter high school classrooms. In the atmosphere of today's war on terror, when color-coded alert levels keep many Americans worried about their everyday safety, many young students have trouble believing that an abstract notion like the Cold War could have seemed threatening. After all, there was no direct fighting. Certainly, attacks on the continental United States itself were not likely.

Such attitudes are a great injustice to the memory of the Cold War. For many, it was a terrifying experience that made people question if they would wake up the next morning or if nuclear holocaust would erupt in the middle of the night. It is difficult to push students, who even today are detached from concern over terrorism, into considering such prolonged stress as significant.

Specifically, students often view the Cuban Missile Crisis as unimportant. They do not understand the significance of missiles so close to the United States, and how seriously this event impacted U.S. policy and the psychological state of everyday Americans.

If possible, gather a few foam tennis balls or other lightweight objects that can be thrown without the danger of inflicting real harm. If no other options are available, loosely crinkled balls of notebook paper will also suffice.

ACTIVITY

Begin with a general discussion of the principles of mutually assured destruction. Make sure students understand the basics of intercontinental ballistic missiles (ICBMs). Point out that unlike in the movies, these are not superaccurate missiles that can travel thousands of miles in an instant. Note the elaborate process necessary to initiate their use, as well as the significant travel time (about 35 minutes at the time of the Cuban Missile Crisis).

Give two students on opposite ends of the room your "missiles," or the balls that you have ready. Identify one as the Soviet Union and the other as the United States. Step back and tell them that one of them must launch within the next ten seconds. Witness that, perhaps after a few pump fakes (which can be exploited in later discussion as close calls), the students will eventually throw at each other.

Be careful to note that once one student throws, the other has ample time to throw his or her own missile before being struck. If a "missile" should go awry and strike another student, exclaim that an innocent country has been attacked! It is easy to push this metaphor very far while still maintaining student interest. Repeat the exercise a few times with different students to give more of them a chance to participate as well as have additional opportunities to discuss how these foam balls relate to actual missiles.

After a few launches, it is time to change things up. Once again, give two students on far sides of the room their "missiles." This time, however, give a third "missile" to a student sitting very near the student designated as the United States. Identify that this new missile-wielding student is the tiny island nation of Cuba, recently outfitted by the Russians with nuclear missiles.

As before, tell the students that they have about ten seconds to launch their weapons. This time, the United States is in much greater trouble. If Cuba launches first, the United States will likely not have time to throw his or her own ball. The student must also decide whether to retaliate against the Soviet Union or against Cuba.

Discuss if President Kennedy did the right thing in so aggressively addressing the Cuban Missile Crisis to prevent the Soviet Union from establishing a nuclear presence in Cuba. Be sure to also address that the United States maintained its own nuclear bases in Turkey.

Extension: Raise the argument that some people believe that if a technology is invented, it will eventually be used, no matter what. Discuss the consequences of this argument in light of the existence of nuclear arms and missiles.

ACTIVITY 62

Listening to Sources?

INTRODUCTION

Music is a huge part of student culture. Naming the past five presidents would be a challenge to most teenagers. Yet ask them to name the last five winners of *American Idol* and they will be able to provide a list of pop stars in an instant. From cell phone ringers to television shows, popular music is spreading everywhere and students all over are taking it all in.

The discipline of history, in its recent past, has adapted to similar changing circumstances. For a long time, historians emphasized only the written word. But the twentieth century's explosion of visual images, especially in the last two decades, forced historians to also center attention on images. Now teachers must do the same when it comes to using music in the classroom.

Some teachers use music for the simple purposes of either settling their students down or establishing a period atmosphere. There are, however, more substantial ways of using music and musical sources in the classroom.

The only material and preparation necessary for this activity is to either photocopy or create an overhead projector sheet of the Lyrics and Text Worksheet included with this activity.

The goal of the activity is to get students to evaluate sources as a resource. The question to the class becomes which of the two sources provided here gives a better description of public opinion in regard to the New Deal.

The letter to the president has an air of respectability and appears more formal and therefore more legitimate. The inclusion of a discussion of banks also lends legitimacy. As a result, most students will casually discard the song as unimportant. This is clearly a mistake; the song offers not only insights unavailable in a strictly business letter, but it also reached many more people and had a substantially larger impact.

ACTIVITY

Have students choose which of the two sources they believe to be more important. Instruct them to construct a list of facts they can draw from their source. After a few moments, ask each student to provide one or two facts to the rest of the class and create a master list for everyone to see. With your students, compare the differences in the two lists. It should become clear to the students that neither a popular song nor an elderly couple's letter is more important and that each offers unique insights.

Extension: Ask students what other songs they know of that may depict emotions surrounding a particular event better than a textbook description.

Lyrics and Text

An Excerpt From a Popular Song From 1936

Just hand me my old Martin, for soon I will be startin'
Back to dear old Charleston, far away.
Since Roosevelt's been re-elected, we'll not be neglected,
We've got Franklin D. Roosevelt back again.

No more breadlines we're glad to say, the donkey won the election day,
No more standing in the blowing, snowing rain;
He's got things in full sway, we're all working and getting our pay,
We've got Franklin D. Roosevelt back again.

Note: Martin = a type of guitar; Donkey = the Democratic Party

A Letter Published by Roosevelt's Supporters as Part of His Election Campaign in 1936

Dear Mr. President:

This is just to let you know that everything is all right now. The man you sent found our house and we went down to the bank with him. The bank agreed to let our loan go on for a while longer. You remember I wrote to you about losing the furniture. Well your man got it back for us. I have never heard of a President like you. My wife and I are old folks and don't amount to much but we join those millions of others in praying for you every night.

God bless you.

ACTIVITY 63

Personal Timelines: A Puzzle?

INTRODUCTION

Wars, presidential elections, economic depressions, and social revolutions are all major events that most students can at least understand as significant. It is easy, however, to overlook the individuals of history—as they play a role either in these big moments or in the minutiae of everyday life. In doing so, students can often underestimate the role that individuals play in the present as well, including themselves.

The Space Shuttle *Challenger* exploding on launch.

ACTIVITY

Have students create a timeline of important recent events such as the *Challenger* or *Columbia* disaster or 9/11 and the destruction of the World Trade Center. Have students write a brief narrative of where they were and what they felt about each of these or similar events.

Extension: Students can ask older members of their family or their community about their memories of events such as the assassination of John F. Kennedy or Martin Luther King, Jr.

ACTIVITY 64

Movies as a Window Into History

INTRODUCTION

Steven Spielberg's *Saving Private Ryan* changed how the youngest generations at the close of the twentieth century thought about World War II. Major motion pictures can introduce history to students in a way never before possible. Lectures, PowerPoint slides, audio clips, even documentaries cannot compare to the unprecedented ability of Hollywood to re-create history in living color. Tremendous amounts of capital have been spent to absorb the audience in the environs of the past, engaging students and citizens to a degree otherwise unapproachable. Studies have cited that nearly half of all Americans note movies and TV programs as the top methods of connecting with the past.

School libraries contain growing collections of historical films, and local movie rental stores are certain to have a generous assortment. The world is, almost literally, at the teacher's fingertips.

Of course, there is a dilemma. For all its value in engaging viewers with the past, cinema is under absolutely no obligation to present accurate history. Writers, directors, and studio executives all have the power to alter their version of history so it better fits the screen or appeals to more audiences. While based on factual events, many historical movies simply use history as a springboard to creating gripping drama.

These two facts combined together—the powerful hold cinema has on America's mind and the trend for historical cinema to be historical fiction—make film a serious threat to scholastic study. Americans are learning a false past, thinking all the while it is accurate.

This activity will require a few resources. First, you will need to select a historical drama for your class to view. You can make your decision based on a host of different criteria (your own taste, recent class topics, classroom vote, etc.).

Once you have selected a film, you must prepare some academic sources that focus on the same topic. These sources can be a chapter or section of a textbook, a journal article, even an outline or summary of a book that you make yourself. Since you will be dividing the class into groups, you will want at least a few different academic works.

ACTIVITY

The first stage of this activity is to show your students the film. Before doing so, make sure to discuss with the class the issues raised above, and instruct them to pay attention to historical details throughout the movie and to write down anything that strikes them as significant or surprising.

Once they have seen the movie, divide students into small groups and give each group an academic source on the topic of the film. Instruct each group to prepare a list of similarities and differences between the film and text.

After they have completed their lists, facilitate a presentation of each group's findings.

Extension: Have students write a treatment or brief description of a historical film that they would like to see made.

ACTIVITY 65

Writing Their Own Script

INTRODUCTION

Few students can resist a good drama, be it a movie, play, or television show. Teachers throughout the country and the globe have begun to incorporate such media into their classrooms. There is, however, another way to use drama as a means for motivating and engaging students.

This activity is much longer than those typically included in this book. The most efficient way to allocate time for students to complete all the necessary preparations will be to allow them a few moments at the conclusion of each class period for a set number of days. This will give them time to spend manageable amounts of preparation time both outside of class and during class time without the project's becoming overwhelming.

Another preparation that will be necessary for this activity is to allow some class time for the students to spend time in the library researching. It is best to schedule a library session a few days after you have introduced the project.

You will also need to decide on a relatively specific period of time or an event (for example, a particular campaign during a war, the Constitutional Convention, or life during the Great Depression).

ACTIVITY

Break students into groups of about four or five. Spend a class introducing the event or time period that the students will be working on, making sure to point them toward helpful

resources focused on that time period. The deeper the background you can provide, the easier it will be for the students to become involved in the project.

Once you have introduced the material, explain the actual project to the students. Each group will be responsible for creating a short (about ten minutes) dramatization of fictional characters during that period. All members of the group will be responsible for portraying a character, and contributions and "screen time" should be as equal as possible. The fictional characters can be based on factual people, but the students should be encouraged to use their imaginations to create sympathetic characters. Still, it is important that students keep their scripts as historically accurate as possible and to include as much researched detail as they can.

Give students time to prepare their topics and develop their characters. After one or two sessions, have each group present their plan to you and make sure that you consider it a feasible theme with potential to be fleshed out. Once everyone is approved, it will be up to the teacher to decide how many sessions will be necessary for the students to develop a finished product.

After all the scripts are completed, set a date when students will put on their shows. Each group should have time to perform its script and to answer questions from the class and teacher after it is over.

Have students discuss how historical events can potentially be altered to create greater drama. For example, they can discuss Emanuel Leutze's famous painting "Washington Crossing the Delaware," which was completed in 1851 and appears on the back of the New Jersey state quarter.

Analyze with students how faithful historical reconstructions are to the actual historical information they are based on. Have them visit the Metropolitan Museum online and examine Leutze's painting. Discuss whether or not the painting actually depicts what Washington's crossing was like or if it is an idealization.

ACTIVITY 66

Writing Obituaries

INTRODUCTION

Obituaries are a common feature of most newspapers. They chronicle our history and the passing of those who have lived and worked in our communities. They are an outstanding source of historical information and a unique type of biographical research.

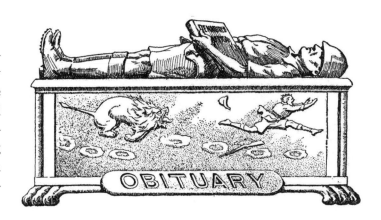

ACTIVITY

Have students search for an obituary of a national figure in a newspaper. It can be a celebrity or someone in politics. They can use a local paper or go online and use the obituary page for a national newspaper such as the *New York Times* (www.nytimes.com/pages/obituaries).

Examples of obituary subjects they can find include all kinds of people, from Queen Victoria to Ray Kroc, the founder of McDonald's.

Assign students a famous figure you are studying in one of your classes (such as Robert E. Lee in American history or William Shakespeare in literature) and have them write an obituary for that person, using a newspaper obituary as a model.

Extension: Have students write their own obituary. In it, they can include information about their lives up to now or what they hope to do or become.

ACTIVITY 67

Take a Trip to Mars

INTRODUCTION

The National Aeronautics and Space Administration (NASA) has been actively researching the planet Mars for several decades. Its activities have included flybys, orbiters, and landings.

ACTIVITY

Have students plan the first manned space mission to Mars. Have them go online and research how long it would take them to travel to the red planet, the types of supplies they would need, and the conditions they would have to create on a spacecraft to make the mission possible. Have them research the conditions they would have to face once they landed on the planet.

A useful Web site where students can start their research is the NASA Mars Exploration Program (http://mars.jpl.nasa.gov).

Results of their research could be incorporated into oral reports, bulletin board displays, Web sites, or even a handbook for Mars exploration.

Extension: Have students conduct a similar project on the outer planets, such as Saturn and Jupiter.

ACTIVITY 68

CIA Fact Book

THE WORLD FACTBOOK

INTRODUCTION

Among the most interesting and useful reference sources available online is the U.S. Central Intelligence Agency's (CIA) *The World Factbook* (www.cia.gov/cia/publications/factbook/index .html). In it are detailed statistics and background essays about every nation in the world.

ACTIVITY

Have students select a country they would like to become an expert on. Have them answer a series of basic questions about the country. (These can be drawn up by you or developed through a classroom discussion.) Students can use the information they gather to create oral and written reports.

Extension: Have students conduct a set of comparisons with a fellow "student expert" on another country. For example, have students present information for comparisons on population, size, economies, and so on between the United States and China or the United States and Canada (U.S. population: 297 million; China's population: 1.3 billion; Canada's population: 33 million).

ACTIVITY 69

Talking to an Expert

INTRODUCTION

Invite a guest to speak to your class on a subject he or she is an expert on. If the person can't come to your class, see if he or she is willing to conduct a "press conference" by speakerphone or even in a "Webinar" (a type of Web conference) or online chat. Have students develop lists of questions that they can ask your guest.

Before students conduct their press conference, discuss what a press conference is like. If at all possible, have them watch a press conference on television or listen to a press conference on the radio.

ACTIVITY

Have students conduct their press conference and then use the information they have collected to issue a press release or to write a newspaper article about the expert and the subject he or she discussed.

Extension: Have students go online to research and create a profile of an expert or well-known person they would like to interview.

ACTIVITY 70

Famous Last Words

INTRODUCTION

Technological inventions often tend to be underestimated. There are many predictions by very capable people that things will not be discovered in the future or that inventions will be of no consequence, which, in the end, turn out to profoundly shape the world.

"Computers in the future may weigh no more than 1.5 tons."

—Popular Mechanics,
forecasting the relentless march of science, 1949

"I think there is a world market for maybe five computers."

—Thomas Watson,
chairman of IBM, 1943

"There is no reason anyone would want a computer in their home."

—Ken Olsen,
president and founder of
Digital Equipment Corp., 1977

"This telephone has too many shortcomings to be seriously considered as a means of communication. The device is inherently of no value to us."

—Western Union internal memo, 1876

"The wireless music box has no imaginable commercial value. Who would pay for a message sent to nobody in particular?"

—David Sarnoff's associates,
in response to his urgings for
investment in the radio in the 1920s

"The concept is interesting and well formed, but in order to earn better than a 'C' the idea must be feasible."

—A Yale University management professor
in response to Fred Smith's paper proposing reliable
overnight delivery service. Smith went on to found Federal Express.

"Who the hell wants to hear actors talk?"

—H. M. Warner,
Warner Brothers, 1927

99

"We don't like their sound, and guitar music is on the way out."

—Decca Recording Co.
rejecting the Beatles, 1962

"Heavier-than-air flying machines are impossible."

—Lord Kelvin,
president, Royal Society, 1895

"Airplanes are interesting toys but of no military value."

—Marechal Ferdinand Foch,
Professor of Strategy, Ecole Superieure de Guerre, 1911

"Everything that can be invented has been invented."

—Charles H. Duell,
Commissioner, U.S. Office of Patents, 1899

ACTIVITY

Have students read the quotes listed above and then discuss why these people's views were so limited.

Extension: Have students go online and research an emerging and radical technology, such as nanotechnology (building machines at a microscopic level), and have them write a brief position paper about why such a technology will, or will not, be important to society.

ACTIVITY 71

Columbus and Culture

Statue of Columbus at the 1893 World's Columbian Exposition.

INTRODUCTION

Have students try to discover how many places the image of Columbus or his name shows up in our culture. For example, consider the names of banks, a river in Washington State, images on postage stamps. Think about events like the 1893 World's Columbian Exposition.

ACTIVITY

As a class activity, have students split into teams and see who can come up with the longest list of examples where Columbus shows up in the culture. Create a master list of these entries, which can be used for class discussion or as the basis for having students create a bulletin board or exhibit. Discuss with students what the different images and uses of Columbus's name represent and/or mean. Do the same exercise with another historical figure such as Lincoln or Washington. Talk with them about the mythic representations of people, the use of these representations, and what these people's actual lives were like. For example, have students analyze why we almost always see George Washington depicted as an old man. What did he look like as a youth? Why isn't he portrayed as a younger man?

Extension: Have students collect examples of where we use historical figures in businesses and advertising (for example, Washington Mutual, Lincoln Trust, etc.).

ACTIVITY 72

Collage

INTRODUCTION

In the mid-1920s, the French artist Yves Tanguy and the poet Jacques Prévert created *Cadavre Exquis* (*Exquisite Corpse*) based on the children's game of Consequences. In the game, people participating drew a body as a shared activity. Each person sketched a separate portion of the body (leg, head, torso, etc.) without seeing what the other people were drawing. Then the parts were put together.

ACTIVITY

This could be done by having people drawing on proportionally premeasured sheets of paper or by marking out the spacing for a body on a large piece of brown paper, making sure that the participants do not see each other's drawings. Once the separate drawings are combined together, they have a surreal quality that can be quite engaging.

Extension: Have students create a "collective" collage in which they construct the picture of a specific object by each taking a turn adding pieces to its construction.

ACTIVITY 73

Making Models

INTRODUCTION

Making models is an effective way of testing out and representing ideas in the real world. Sometimes these models can deal with complex ideas in philosophy or mathematics. For example, the German founder of the kindergarten movement, Friedrich Froebel (1782–1852) created many educational devices and activities for children, including a device made up of a wooden sphere approximately three inches in diameter; a wooden cube; and wooden cylinder.

The toy physically demonstrated the dialectical principle of the German philosopher Georg Wilhelm Friedrich Hegel (1770–1831). According to Hegel's theory, "Thesis and antithesis yields synthesis." Thus, seemingly opposite things can be "synthesized" or combined together through the dialectic process to create a new unity. In the case of the sphere, all sides of the object are round. In the case of the cube, all sides are flat. By combining these two seemingly opposite objects, a synthesis is achieved in the form of the cylinder, which includes both flat and rounded sides—thus providing a tangible demonstration of the dialectical process.

Computer programs, particularly simulations such as *SimCity* or *SimEarth*, provide models of real-world experiences.

ACTIVITY

Have students brainstorm in groups to see if they can invent a model to represent an idea, concept, or event. For example, have students try to create a model for lava bubbling in a volcano (pea soup bubbling in a pot on top of a stove).

Extension: Discuss with students how a metaphor ("her eyes were blue as the ocean") serves as a model to describe an object or thing.

ACTIVITY 74

The World Without Human Life

INTRODUCTION

Human beings tend to be pretty proud of themselves. We celebrate our existence in myths, religious texts, and a wide range of philosophies. We act like the world and its plants, minerals, and animals belong to us and that we can do pretty much whatever we want with them.

ACTIVITY

Have students research how old the earth is and how long life on earth is believed to have existed. Have them discuss and write about how the world would be different if human beings did not exist. Would the earth be a better place or worse off without human beings?

Extension: Have students discuss whether or not there are animals other than humans who occupy the entire planet. Assuming that humans are unique in this regard, discuss with students what the significance of this concept might be.

ACTIVITY 75

Creating the Scene for a Story

INTRODUCTION

Fiction writers use their imaginations to create environments in which their stories take place. Many situations for their stories are often based on an actual place. Jane Austen used the English countryside and towns such as London and Bath for her stories. For his novel *A Room With a View*, E. M. Forster used Florence, Italy, as the setting for his story.

ACTIVITY

Have students take an actual place (Central Park in New York City, the Parthenon in Athens, the Eiffel Tower in Paris, for example) and develop a description or "treatment" of three to four pages for its use in a story. This treatment should include as much detail as possible. Students can learn more about the setting they are interested in by visiting Web sites about it online or by researching it from traditional book and photographic sources.

Extension: Have students find a location in their neighborhood or town and use it as the basis for the development of a treatment.

ACTIVITY 76

How Long Is a Thousand Years?

INTRODUCTION

The passage of historical time is something that students often have difficulty relating to. They can obtain something of a sense of the magnitude and scope of time by doing the following exercise.

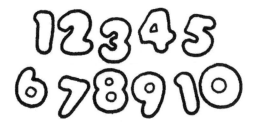

ACTIVITY

Have students write down their age and quietly count it out aloud. Next have them do the same for the age of one of their parents and then one of their grandparents.

Now have them count back the years to the Vietnam War, to the American Revolution, and so on. Have them count out a thousand years as an assignment, making a mark and crossing them in five-year intervals to keep track. (Have them turn in this assignment to make sure that they don't simply claim they have counted out a thousand years.)

Talk with students about what counting out the years felt like, whether it was difficult or tedious and whether it seemed to take a long time.

Extension: Have students explore how time is recorded and kept track of in our culture. Discuss what life would be like without clocks and watches.

ACTIVITY 77

Creating a Dadaist Poem

INTRODUCTION

Dadaism was a literary and artistic movement from the period around World War I. Its leaders included artists and writers such as Tristan Tzara, Hugo Ball, Hans Arp, and Richard Huelsenbeck. As an artistic movement, Dadaism stressed unconscious elements, irrationalism, irreverent wit, and spontaneity.

Tristan Tzara created an interesting technique for making poems based on Dadaist principles, described in detail in the following "Recipe for a Dadaist Poem" (1920):

Take a newspaper.
Take a pair of scissors.
Choose an article as long as you are planning to make your poem.
Cut out the article.
Then cut out each of the words that make up this article and put them in the bag.
Shake it gently.
Then take the scraps one after the other in the order in which they left the bag.
Copy conscientiously.
This poem will be like you.

ACTIVITY

Have students create their own Dadaist poems using an existing article or by having them create a word list or series of sentences, which they cut up and use to create poems. Have them snip out images from magazines that are of interest to them that can also be randomly selected, using the same technique, to create collages of words and images.

Extension: Have students use a number selection system (every fifth word in a passage from a famous author, for example) to choose a word. Have them write these words down and then have them fill in words in between to create a story, narrative, or poem.

ACTIVITY 78

War Stories

The raising of the American flag by U.S. Marines atop Mount Suribachi during the Battle of Iwo Jima is a well-know image in American history. This photograph was actually of a second flag raising after the battle and was taken by the Associated Press photographer Joe Rosenthal, Courtesy of the National Archives.

INTRODUCTION

Oral history involves interviewing people about their lives and the events they have lived through. Every community has military veterans, and their stories are often of particular interest.

109

ACTIVITY

Have students conduct an oral history interview with someone who has served in a war as a member of the military. Have students ask questions such as the following:

1. What war were you a part of?

2. How did you become involved in the military?

3. What did you do?

4. What was your best experience?

5. What was your worst experience?

6. How do you feel about having served in the war now that it is over? (Or now that you are out of the military?)

7. Did your experience in the military shape you in important ways? If so, how?

Students can consult many online sources as models in developing their interviews. Among the most valuable is the Veterans History Project at the Library of Congress (www.loc.gov/vets).

Provided that appropriate permission is obtained from the people they interview, students can post interviews online as transcripts, audio files, or both. Information from interviews can be integrated into larger research reports, or students can create individual profiles of individuals and their experiences. Information about ethical issues, permission forms, and related procedures in doing oral histories can be found at the following online addresses: Step-by-Step Guide to Oral History (www.dohistory.org/on_your_own/toolkit/oralHistory.html) and Oral History Association (www.dickinson.edu/oha).

Extension: Have students find collections of oral histories available online and use them as the basis for creating a report or research paper.

ACTIVITY 79

Editorial Cartoons as Social Commentary

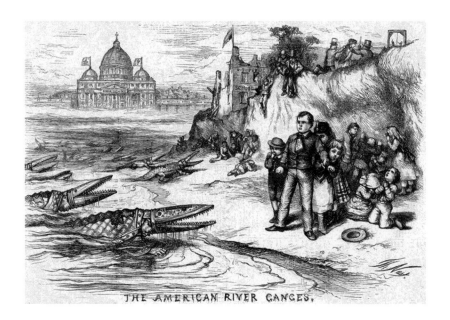

THE AMERICAN RIVER GANGES.

INTRODUCTION

One of the most famous editorial cartoons of the nineteenth century is Thomas Nast's May 1875 depiction in *Harper's Weekly* of Catholic bishops invading the United States and taking over the American public school system (illustrated above). The cartoon is an invaluable source for understanding anti-Catholic sentiment in the United States after the Civil War. Editorial cartoons are incredible sources for helping students understand political and social commentary.

ACTIVITY

Have students find a political cartoon on a current issue that is of interest to them (Supreme Court nominations, privacy rights, free speech, flag burning). Have them research the topic in more detail using the library and the Internet and write a brief report (one–three pages) on the issue addressed in a cartoon of their choice.

   An outstanding resource for contemporary editorial cartoon material is Daryl Cagel's Professional Cartoonist Index (www.cagle.com).

   Students should place the cartoon at the beginning of the report. Reports can be presented by students in class and discussed.

Extension: Students can create a bulletin board display of their favorite cartoons or a display that focuses on a single issue (women's rights, civil rights, or some aspect of local politics).

ACTIVITY 80

True or False

INTRODUCTION

Construct a list of statements that are true or false. For example, "The United States, because of its excellent health care system, has the lowest infant mortality rate in the world." (False: Our infant mortality rate is 6.5 per 1,000 live births. Singapore's is nearly three times better at 2.29 per 1,000 live births.) "Walking along the edge of the coastline of the continental United States is equivalent to walking halfway around the world at the Equator. (True: The coastline of the continental United States is 12,380 miles, or 19,924 kilometers long.)

TRUE or FALSE

ACTIVITY

Have students research in the library and online to see which of the statements in the introduction to this activity are true and which are false. Have them construct other true/false items for students to be tested on. See if students can surprise one another with information and facts that they would not expect to be true or false.

Extension: Use the statements in the introduction as the basis for class discussions (e.g., "If we are the richest country in the world, why don't we have the best health care system?").

ACTIVITY 81

Creating Codes

INTRODUCTION

Codes can be created in many different ways. One of the most interesting is to use a rule-based system. For example, take all the vowels out of a word, just leaving the consonants, and then add a hyphen where each vowel has been removed. Remove the space between the words. An example can be seen in the following sentence:

The dog jumped over the fence.

Using a vowel subtraction code, the sentence would look like this:

Th-d-gj-mp-d-v-r h-f-nc-.

ACTIVITY

Have students experiment with creating their own unique codes by including vowel subtraction or letter swapping (a = b, b = a), by substituting numbers for letters, or writing backward.
Discuss why the use of codes can be fun and useful.

Extension: Have students go online and explore how urban graffiti often has coded messages included in it.

ACTIVITY 82

What Is the Law?

INTRODUCTION

After World War II, people argued about whether or not the laws of the Nazi Third Reich were legitimate. The legal theorist Lon Fuller believed, for example, that a legal system devoted to evil purposes could not be considered valid.

ACTIVITY

Have students discuss what constitutes a good law and what could be considered a bad law. Is it possible for a law to be both good and bad?

Extension: Have students draft a law that they think would be good for society. Students can do this as part of a group activity or as an individual writing assignment. The law they create should include a paragraph explaining why it is needed and then a precise phrasing of the law.

ACTIVITY 83

When Is the Law the Law?

INTRODUCTION

The Declaration of Independence demanded that the British colonists be provided with legal rights including "life, liberty and the pursuit of happiness." At the time of the American Revolution, this excluded people of African American descent. In addition, women (of all races) were given only abridged rights. Women could not vote, for example, until 1921.

Are there circumstances when it can be legitimately argued that certain groups should have fewer rights than other groups? Have students list examples of laws that abridge the freedom (or rights) of some groups over others. An example would be individuals not being allowed to drive an automobile until they are sixteen.

ACTIVITY

Have students discuss whether there are rights that apply to all people equally. Have them write a law, individually or as a group, that calls for a "universal principal," such as education for all.

Discuss the refinement of the law. For example, should a universal right to education be a basic human right?

Extension: Have students explore laws that have discriminated against different historical groups (e.g., slave and Black codes).

ACTIVITY 84

Symbols in Our Culture

INTRODUCTION

Symbols are found throughout our culture. They are on our money, in advertisements, on street signs, and on television. Have students create a list of symbols that represent the United States of America or our people (eagle, Liberty, Liberty Bell, flag, and so on).

ACTIVITY

Have the students choose a symbol that represents the United States and research its history. Who created it? When? Why? Have them design a symbol that represents the American people in the 21st century.

Extension: Discuss with students how a symbol that had previously been considered in a positive way can take on negative overtones. The swastika, for example, is an ancient symbol of good luck in India. After the Nazi Party in Germany adopted it, the swastika eventually took on a very different meaning for many people all over the world.

ACTIVITY 85

Symbols on Our Money

INTRODUCTION

Symbols are found on most of our money. They provide clues as to what values we hold as a nation and what our history has been.

ACTIVITY

Have students look at a dollar bill and identify the symbols included on it (the American eagle, the Seal of the United States, the Eye of God and the pyramid, and so on). On the back of a Mercury dime, they can find a *fasces* (an ax and a bundle of sticks), which is a traditional symbol of the Roman Republic.

Extension: Have students create a bulletin board or a Web site that describes the meaning of symbols found on our money. Then have them look at money from other types of symbolic representations or at the money from other countries.

ACTIVITY 86

What's on the Stamp?

INTRODUCTION

Postage stamps include a wide range of information on topics such as history, science, and art.

ACTIVITY

Have students discuss what types of topics are found on postage stamps. Have them look at examples of different postage stamps created both in the United States and in other countries. Examples can be found by searching online using search terms such as "American stamps," "foreign stamps," and so on.

Extension: Have students design their own stamps. Assign them the task of creating a historical stamp or a stamp celebrating a subject such as flowers, a famous musician, or an event.

ACTIVITY 87

Place Names

INTRODUCTION

People have a tendency to take the names of their states for granted. Some names are obvious, such as New Mexico. But did you know that the name for North Carolina (formally a British colony known as Carolina) is a reference to British royalty (King Charles)?

ACTIVITY

Have each student research the meaning of the names of two states.

Extension: Have students research other historical names that play a role in geography. Where do city names such as San Francisco, St. Louis, and St. Paul come from? What about names like Kalamazoo, Miami, and Cherokee Gap?

ACTIVITY 88

Art Museums of the World

Museum of Art

INTRODUCTION

Most major art museums have Web sites that include not only current exhibits but extensive catalogues of their major holdings. It is possible to tour online most of the major art collections of the world, from the Metropolitan Museum in New York City to the Louvre in Paris to the Tate Gallery in London.

ACTIVITY

Have each student choose a different museum and visit it online. Have each student construct a tour of the museum and some of its major holdings in the form of a bulletin board display, a written report, or a PowerPoint presentation.

Extension: Have students construct a personal museum, based solely on works they like or think are important. This personal museum can be created in the form of a notebook, a PowerPoint presentation, or a Web site.

ACTIVITY 89

America's Attic

INTRODUCTION

The Smithsonian Institution in Washington, D.C., was founded in 1846 as the result of a grant from James Smithson (1765–1829). Today, the Smithsonian Institution is made up of a wide range of museums, most of which are located in Washington, D.C., including the Air and Space Museum, the National Gallery of Art, and the Holocaust Museum.

ACTIVITY

Have students visit the Web site for the Smithsonian Institution. Have them explore the different museums and choose a museum about which to develop a report, a bulletin board exhibit, or a PowerPoint presentation.

Extension: Students can be put together in groups, go online, and create a virtual field trip to the Smithsonian.

ACTIVITY 90

Written in Stone

INTRODUCTION

Cemeteries and tombstones are outstanding resources for understanding local history. Memorialized within these sacred grounds are the people—both famous and not so famous—who have shaped our history.

The Old Granary, which was founded in 1660 and is Boston's third oldest cemetery, includes the graves of the following figures from the Revolutionary period: Samuel Adams (1722–1803), statesman; Crispus Attucks (1723–1770), slave, Boston Massacre victim; John Hancock (1737–1793), statesman; James Otis (1725–1783), lawyer, Revolutionary War patriot; and Paul Revere (1735–1818), silversmith and patriot.

Cemeteries can have much more recent histories as well. Los Angeles has many important cemeteries with famous celebrities interred in them. For example, Forest Lawn–Hollywood Hills Cemetery is the resting place for Liberace, Buster Keaton, and Bette Davis. Hollywood Forever Cemetery, Los Angeles, has the remains of Mel Blanc, Rudolph Valentino, Bugsy Siegel, and John Huston. Westwood Village Memorial Park Cemetery has the graves of Marilyn Monroe, Frank Zappa, Billy Wilder, and Natalie Wood.

Wikipedia, the online encyclopedia, has an outstanding listing of cemeteries in the United States at the following address: http://en.wikipedia.org/wiki/List_of_cemeteries_in_the_United_States.

ACTIVITY

Have students visit a local cemetery to learn about architecture, local history, and stone masonry. Have them consider what other things they can learn from their local cemeteries. What about religious practices and traditions as well as community values?

Students can write a report about a local cemetery, including its history and the people who are buried there. They can profile the grave and the life of a single famous person or of someone who was not so famous.

Extension: Have students photograph and catalog architectural features of a local cemetery. Often, some of the most interesting sculptures in a city will be found in one of its historic cemeteries.

ACTIVITY 91

Photographic Community Timeline

INTRODUCTION

Having students create a historical photographic timeline for a specific period of time can help make the past become much more tangible and real. Depending on their community, they can find images in local history books that they can photocopy. They may also be able to find images on Web sites about their community (local historical societies often have excellent collections of photographs online).

ACTIVITY

Make sure that students record the dates and captions for the photographs they have collected. Have them use these photographs as the basis for creating timelines of their communities. The timelines can be put up on a bulletin board, pasted to rolls of shelf paper, and taped to a wall or put into a notebook.

Destitute pea pickers in California. Mother of seven children. Age thirty-two. Photograph by Dorothea Lange, February 1936. Courtesy of the Library of Congress.

Extension: Have students collect photographs of their community during the Great Depression to use as the basis of a timeline. Photographs of the Great Depression are available for most communities throughout the United States through the Library of Congress. Visit the following Web sites to find more examples: America From the Great Depression to World War II: Black and White Photographs From the FSA-OWI, 1935–1945 (http://memory.loc.gov/ammem/fsahtml/fahome.html).

ACTIVITY 92

The Sounds of Silence

INTRODUCTION

This is a fun activity that can get students inspired to write a narrative or story when they don't think they can.

ACTIVITY

Record a television program that your students are likely to watch. Explain to them that, as a writing assignment, they are going to write the dialogue for a five-minute segment of the program. They will do this by watching the segment you have chosen with the sound turned off. Using their imaginations, they can create whatever dialogue they want, as long as it suits the action in the segment of the program.

This can be done as a group activity in which students create their dialogue with one another. An interesting experiment could involve having different groups of students watch different segments of the same program and then paste together the dialogues they create in order to make an entire program. If you have tape- and sound-editing capabilities, you might want to have students create the dialogue for an entire episode of a television program.

Extension: Have students do the same activity by sitting in a public place and making a recording of people passing by and then creating a dialogue or narrative based on what they have recorded.

ACTIVITY 93

What's in a Name?

INTRODUCTION

Have you ever thought about what is in a name? For example, women in much of Western culture are given their husband's last name when they get married. What does this imply? What does it mean when a woman keeps her maiden name? Is this a good thing, or does it just not matter? Should children be given the last names of their mothers rather than their fathers? In Hispanic cultures, children often get the names of both parents

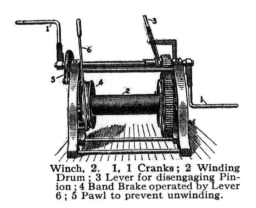

Winch, 2. 1, 1 Cranks; 2 Winding Drum; 3 Lever for disengaging Pinion; 4 Band Brake operated by Lever 6; 5 Pawl to prevent unwinding.

(e.g., Lopez-Gottardi, Garcia-Henandez). With a hyphenated name, should the name of the father or the mother come first? Why? Does it make any difference?

ACTIVITY

Have students explore whether or not their surname has a specific meaning. For example, the common name *Smith* probably refers to someone who has a relative that was a blacksmith. The name *Wheelwright* refers to a wagon or wheel maker, and the name *Baker* obviously is based on someone who made bread or pastries.

Extension: Have students interview members of their family about where their name came from. Have them find out the first, last, and middle names of all of their parents and grandparents and write a brief report outlining the history and meaning of their family names.

ACTIVITY 94

More What's in a Name?

"At the Bus Station," Durham, North Carolina. Photograph by Jack Delano, May 1940. Courtesy of the Library of Congress.

INTRODUCTION

What we call people can tell us a lot about their history and experience. Think for a moment about people of African American origin. They have been referred to as *Colored, Black,* and *African American.* What is the difference in meaning of each term? Why is one term used during one historical period to describe African American people but not used later on?

What about terms used to describe people of Hispanic origins? What is the difference between *Latino* and *Hispanic* or between *Latina* and *Latino*?

ACTIVITY

Have students discuss, either as a whole-class activity or in groups, the use of different terms to describe who or what they are. Explore the distinctions between ethnic and racial categories. For example, are African Americans ethnics? What defines ethnicity?

ACTIVITY 95

Crazy Inventions

INTRODUCTION

Inventions and the patents for them are not always serious. Often, they represent crazy things people invent just for fun or that they think may be more useful than they really are. Imagine an electric ice cream cone or a hat with an electric fan that filters the smoke from cigarettes or cigars. These are just a few of the crazy inventions that actually have patents on them from the U.S. Patent Office.

ACTIVITY

Have students think of a crazy invention to patent—maybe a pen with a fan built into it to keep a person cool or a sail on the back of a bicycle. Have students make a drawing of their invention and write a two- or three-paragraph description of how it works and why it is a useful invention.

Extension: Discuss with students inventions that have changed the world (the electric lightbulb, the atom bomb, and so on) and what our world would be like without them.

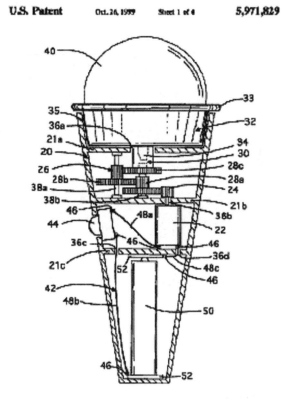

U.S. Patent   Oct. 26, 1999   Sheet 1 of 4   5,971,829

U.S. Patent 5971829: A novelty amusement eating receptacle for supporting, rotating, and sculpting a portion of ice cream or similarly malleable food while it is being consumed, comprising a handheld housing, a rotatable cup supported by the handheld housing and adapted to receive and contain a portion of ice cream or food product of similar consistency, and a drive mechanism in the handheld housing for imparting rotation on the cup and rotationally feeding its contents against a person's outstretched tongue.

ACTIVITY 96

Idioms

INTRODUCTION

Idioms involve a special use of words in language—that is, words with meanings based on a story or image. In English, for example, we use the term "sour grapes" to refer to people who say they don't care about something that they may very much care about. For example, a friend of yours might say, "I don't really care that I wasn't invited to the party." Now you know that he or she really did want to go to the party, and you say to yourself, "sour grapes." The term comes from Aesop's fable "The Fox and the Grapes," in which a fox tries to jump up and get a bunch of grapes off a vine but cannot reach them. Discouraged, he walks away saying: "Oh they probably were sour anyway and not worth eating."

ACTIVITY

Have students create a list of ten idioms (examples: "Getting out on the wrong side of the bed." "Slow but sure wins the race."). Be prepared to discuss how the use of idioms enriches language but also makes it difficult for people learning a new language to understand what is being said or written by others.

Extension: Discuss with students where idioms come from and why they are so common in our language.

ACTIVITY 97

Famous Inventions and Their Impact on the World

INTRODUCTION

We tend to take for granted the inventions that surround us in our day-to-day lives. Yet different inventions profoundly affect the world and how we live in it. Think for a moment about how your life would be different if no one had invented the automobile, the lightbulb, or the airplane.

ACTIVITY

Have students answer the question, What is the most important invention in your day-to-day life and why? Have them write a two-page essay that can be used as a starting point for discussion in class explaining what their lives would be like without the invention of the lightbulb and the automobile.

Extension: Have students discuss how computers are the basis for other inventions. Explore with them how certain inventions and technologies would not be possible without the underlying technology provided by computers. Use as an example cell phone technology or the space shuttle.

ACTIVITY 98

What Is in Good Taste?

INTRODUCTION

Different cultures interpret things as being in "good taste" differently. This applies to what is beautiful, what is good to eat, and so on. In certain parts of China, caterpillar larvae are fried and eaten with vegetables. Diving beetles and silk worms are also eaten in China.

ACTIVITY

Ask students if they think eating bugs is gross. The response will almost certainly be yes. Ask them if they like eating a steak. What about beef tongue or organ meats such as brains, liver, or sweet breads (pancreas)? Discuss with them whether eating a steak (part of a cow's thigh) is actually any more gross than eating a cow's tongue. (Be advised not to have this discussion before lunch.)

Next, have students find a painting from a book or an Internet source that they think is beautiful. Have them find one they think is ugly. Have them bring copies to class and discuss which one is beautiful for them and which one is not.

Extension: Have students complete a writing assignment in which they outline ten things that make something beautiful. These ideas can be developed as part of a group discussion or on an individual basis. Individual points can be combined together to create a class "manifesto" defining the criteria for what is beautiful or tasteful from an artistic perspective.

ACTIVITY 99

Creating a Self-Portrait

INTRODUCTION

"Who am I?" is a question everybody asks about themselves at some point in their lives. Artists, both writers and painters, have asked this question and expressed themselves in many different media. The French painter, Paul Gauguin (1848–1903), for example, created a wonderful portrait of himself in 1889 for the dining room of an inn in Le Pouldu, France. This self-portrait is now part of the collection of the National Gallery in Washington, D.C. Print a copy of the portrait or show it to students on a computer monitor. Review with the students the different elements in this self-portrait. What about the halo over his head, the snake (a symbol of temptation and also of knowledge), and a pair of apples (a reference to the fruit of knowledge and the Fall from the Garden of Eden)? What is this portrait actually about? What does it mean? And what does it tell us about Gauguin as a man and how he saw himself?

Paul Gauguin, *Self-Portrait*, 1889. Courtesy of the National Gallery of Art.

ACTIVITY

Have students create their own self-portraits, not simply making pictures of themselves but using symbols and objects to express who and what they are.

Extension: Have students write a poem about themselves or, if they like, one that describes another person.

ACTIVITY 100

Found Art

INTRODUCTION

"Found art" or *found objects* (*objet trouvé* in French) are works of art created from things that originally had a more practical function. Also known as "ready made" art, the idea was first introduced by the French artist Marcel Duchamp (1887–1968). Duchamp, for example, in 1913 took a bicycle wheel and attached it to the top of a wooden stool to create a sculpture titled *Bicycle Wheel*. One of Duchamp's most famous pieces is his *Fountain* and is simply a urinal that he found in a plumbing store that he signed with the pseudonym "R. Mutt." This piece, when it was introduced as an exhibit in 1917, shocked the art world. The debate still rages as to whether or not it is really art. Another famous example of found art is that done by Pablo Picasso (1881–1973), who combined a bicycle saddle with handlebars to create a bull's head. Tracey Emin (b. 1963–), an English artist, has a work titled *My Bed* made from her unmade bed with its rumpled sheets and pillows.

ACTIVITY

Have students discuss whether found art is actually art. Does found art need to be modified to become a work of art? Can giving an object a title change its meaning? For example, can someone take a teenager's car and paint the word *Freedom* on its side and in doing so make it a piece of art?

Extension: Have students take a found object and make it into a work of art. Have them organize an exhibit of their works of art as a shared activity.

References

Abowitz, K. (2005). Confronting the paradox of autonomy in a social foundations classroom. In D. W. Butin (Ed.), *Teaching social foundations of education: Contexts, theories, and issues* (pp. 127–150). Mahwah, NJ: Erlbaum.

Basso, K. (2000). Stalking with stories. In B. A. Levinson (Ed.), *Schooling the symbolic animal: Social and cultural dimensions of education* (pp. 41–52). Lanham, MD: Rowman & Littlefield.

Bateson, G. (2000). *Steps to an ecology of mind.* Chicago: University of Chicago Press.

Bransford, J. (2000). *How people learn: Brain, mind, experience, and school.* Washington, D.C.: National Academy Press.

Brown, J. S., Collins, A., & Durgid, P. (1989). Situated cognition and the culture of learning. *Educational Researcher, 18*(1), 32–41.

Butin, D. W. (2005). Identity (re)construction and student resistance. In D. W. Butin (Ed.), *Teaching social foundations of education: Contexts, theories, and issues.* Mahwah, NJ: Erlbaum.

Chase, W. G., & Simon, H. A. (1973). Perception in chess. *Cognitive Psychology, 1,* 33–81.

Clarke, A. (1984). *Profiles of the future: An inquiry into the limits of the possible.* New York: Holt, Rinehart & Winston.

Cuban, L. (1992). *How teachers taught: Constancy and change in American classrooms, 1890–1990.* New York: Teachers College Press.

DeGroot, A. D. (1965). *Thought and choice in chess.* The Hague, The Netherlands: Mouton Press.

Dewey, J. (1910). *How we think.* Boston: D. C. Heath.

Dickson, D. B. Jr. (1992). W. E. B. Du Bois and the idea of double consciousness. *American Literature: A Journal of Literary History, Criticism, and Bibliography, 64*(2), 299–309.

Du Bois, W. E. B. (1907). *The souls of Black folks: Essays and sketches* (7th ed.). Chicago: McClurg.

Ericsson, K., Chase, W., & Faloon, S. (1980). Acquisition of a memory skill. *Science, 208,* 1181–1182.

Fish, S. (2005, May 31). Devoid of content. *New York Times,* p. A19.

Gardner, H. (2004). *Changing minds: The art and science of changing our own and other people's minds.* Cambridge, MA: Harvard Business School Press.

Geertz, C. (1973). *The interpretation of cultures: Selected essays.* New York: Basic Books.

Goodlad, J. (1984). *A place called school.* New York: McGraw-Hill.

hooks, B. (1994). *Teaching to transgress: Education as the practice of freedom.* New York: Routledge.

Huberman, M. (1993). The model of the independent artisan in teachers' professional relations. In J. W. Little & M. W. McLaughlin (Eds.), *Teachers' work: Individuals, colleagues, and contexts* (pp. 11–50). New York: Teachers College Press.

Jackson, P. (1990). *Life in classrooms.* New York: Teachers College Press.

Library of Congress. First Flight. *American Memory, Today in History Collection, December 17.* Retrieved December 4, 2007, from http://memory.loc.gov/ammem/today/dec17.html

Meier, D. (2002). *The power of their ideas.* Boston: Beacon Hill Press.

Saxe, J. G. (1873). *The poems of John Godfrey Saxe.* Boston: James R. Osgood.

Schwartz, D. L., Lin, X., Brophy, S., & Bransford, J. D. (2003). Toward the development of flexibly adaptive instructional designs. In C. M. Reigelut (Ed.), *Instructional design theories and models: A new paradigm of instructional theory* (Vol. 2, pp. 183–214). Hillsdale, NJ: Erlbaum.

Wiggins, G. P., & McTighe, J. (1998). *Understanding by design.* Alexandria, VA: Association for Supervision and Curriculum Development.

Zinn, H. (1980). *A people's history of the United States.* New York: Harper & Row.

Zinn, H., with Macedo, D. (2005). *Howard Zinn on democratic education.* Boulder, CO: Paradigm.

**CORWIN
PRESS**

The Corwin Press logo—a raven striding across an open book—represents the union of courage and learning. Corwin Press is committed to improving education for all learners by publishing books and other professional development resources for those serving the field of PreK–12 education. By providing practical, hands-on materials, Corwin Press continues to carry out the promise of its motto: **"Helping Educators Do Their Work Better."**